Marianne Moore was born in Kirkwood, Missouri, in 1887. She attended Bryn Mawr College, and spent her adult life in New York City, in Manhattan and Brooklyn. She was the author of numerous books of poems, including most notably *Observations* (1924), *Selected Poems* (1935), *The Pangolin and Other Verse* (1936), *What Are Years* (1941), and *Collected Poems* (1951). Her lifelong practice of radically innovative formal verse, committed to moral courage and spiritual clarity, won her most of the major poetry awards available to an American: the Bollingen Prize (1951), the National Book Award (1952), the Pulitzer Prize (1952), the American Academy of Arts and Letters Gold Medal (1953), the Robert Frost Medal from the Poetry Society of America (1967), and the National Medal for Literature (1968). She died on 5 February 1972.

MARIANNE MOORE

Selected Poems

with an introduction by T. S. Eliot

FABER & FABER

First published in 1935
by Faber & Faber Ltd
Bloomsbury House
74–77 Great Russell Street
London WC1B 3DA
This edition first published in 2019

Typeset by Typo•glyphix, Burton-on-Trent, DE14 3HE
Printed in England by CPI Group (UK) Ltd, Croydon, CR0 4YY

A CIP record for this book is available from the British Library

ISBN 978-0-571-35114-5

10 9 8 7 6 5 4 3 2 1

Introduction

We know very little about the value of the work of our contemporaries, almost as little as we know about our own. It may have merits which exist only for contemporary sensibility; it may have concealed virtues which will only become apparent with time. How it will rank when we are all dead authors ourselves we cannot say with any precision. If one is to talk about one's contemporaries at all, therefore, it is important to make up our minds as to what we can affirm with confidence, and as to what must be a matter of doubting conjecture. The last thing, certainly, that we are likely to know about them is their 'greatness', or their relative distinction or triviality in relation to the standard of 'greatness'. For in greatness are involved moral and social relations, relations which can only be perceived from a remoter perspective, and which may be said even to be created in the process of history: we cannot tell, in advance, what any poetry is going to do, how it will operate upon later generations. But the *genuineness* of poetry is something which we have some warrant for believing that a small number, but only a small number, of contemporary readers can recognise. I say positively only a small number, because it seems probable that when any poet conquers a really large public in his lifetime, an increasing proportion of his admirers will admire him for extraneous reasons. Not necessarily for bad reasons, but because he becomes known merely as a symbol, in giving a kind of stimulation, or consolation, to his readers, which is a function of his peculiar relation to them in time. Such effect upon contemporary readers may be a legitimate and proper result of some great poetry, but it has been also the result of much ephemeral poetry.

It does not seem to matter much whether one has to struggle with an age which is unconscious and self-satisfied, and therefore hostile to new forms of poetry, or with one like the present which is self-conscious and distrustful of itself, and avid for new forms which will give it status and self-respect. For many modern readers any superficial novelty of form is evidence of, or is as good as, newness of sensibility; and if the sensibility is fundamentally dull and second-hand, so much the better; for there is no quicker way of catching an immediate, if transient, popularity, than to serve stale goods in new packages. One of the tests – though it be only a negative test – of anything really new and genuine, seems to be its capacity for exciting aversion among 'lovers of poetry'.

I am aware that prejudice makes me underrate certain authors: I see them rather as public enemies than as subjects for criticism; and I dare say that a different prejudice makes me uncritically favourable to others. I may even admire the right authors for the wrong reasons. But I am much more confident of my appreciation of the authors whom I admire, than of my depreciation of the authors who leave me cold or who exasperate me. And in asserting that what I call *genuineness* is a more important thing to recognise in a contemporary than *greatness*, I am distinguishing between his function while living and his function when dead. Living, the poet is carrying on that struggle for the maintenance of a living language, for the maintenance of its strength, its subtlety, for the preservation of quality of feeling, which must be kept up in every generation; dead, he provides standards for those who take up the struggle after him. Miss Moore is, I believe, one of those few who have done the language some service in my lifetime.

So far back as my memory extends, which is to the pages of *The Egoist* during the War, and of *The Little Review* and *The Dial* in the years immediately following, Miss Moore has no immediate poetic derivations. I cannot, therefore, fill up my pages with the usual account of influences and development. There is one early poem, *A Talisman*, not reprinted in the text of this volume, which I will quote in full here, because it suggests a slight influence of H.D., certainly of H.D. rather than of any other 'Imagist':

> Under a splintered mast
> Torn from the ship and cast
>   Near her hull,
>
> A stumbling shepherd found
> Embedded in the ground,
>   A sea-gull
>
> Of lapis-lazuli,
> A scarab of the sea,
>   With wings spread—
>
> Curling its coral feet,
> Parting its beak to greet
>   Men long dead.

The sentiment is commonplace, and I cannot see what a bird carved of *lapis-lazuli* should be doing with *coral* feet; but even here the cadence, the use of rhyme, and a certain authoritativeness of manner distinguish the poem. Looking at Miss Moore's poems of a slightly later period, I should say that she had taken to heart the repeated reminder of Mr Pound: that poetry should be as well written as prose. She seems to have saturated her mind in the perfections of prose, in its precision rather than its purple; and to have found her rhythm, her poetry, her appreciation of the individual word, for herself.

The first aspect in which Miss Moore's poetry is likely to strike the reader is that of minute detail rather than that of emotional unity. The gift for detailed observation, for finding the exact words for some experience of the eye, is liable to disperse the attention of the relaxed reader. The minutiae may even irritate the unwary, or arouse in them only the pleasurable astonishment evoked by the carved ivory ball with eleven other balls inside it, the full-rigged ship in a bottle, the skeleton of the crucifix-fish. The bewilderment consequent upon trying to follow so alert an eye, so quick a process of association, may produce the effect of some 'metaphysical' poetry. To the moderately intellectual the poems may appear to be intellectual exercises; only to those whose intellection moves more easily will they immediately appear to have emotional value. But the detail has always its service to perform to the whole. The similes are there for use; as the mussel-shell 'opening and shutting itself like an injured fan' (where *injured* has an ambiguity good enough for Mr Empson), the waves 'as formal as the scales on a fish'. They make us see the object more clearly, though we may not understand immediately why our attention has been called to this object, and though we may not immediately grasp its association with a number of other objects. So, in her amused and affectionate attention to animals – from the domestic cat, or 'to popularize the mule', to the most exotic strangers from the tropics, she succeeds at once in startling us into an unusual awareness of visual patterns, with something like the fascination of a high-powered microscope.

Miss Moore's poetry, or most of it, might be classified as 'descriptive' rather than 'lyrical' or 'dramatic'. Descriptive poetry is supposed to be dated to a period, and to be condemned thereby; but it is really one of the permanent modes of expression. In the eighteenth century – or say a period which includes *Cooper's Hill*, *Windsor Forest*, and Gray's *Elegy* – the scene described is a point of departure for meditations on one thing or another. The poetry of the Romantic Age, from Byron at his worst to Wordsworth at his best, wavers between the reflective and the evocative; but the description, the picture set before you, is always there for the same purpose. The aim of 'imagism', so far as I understand it, or so far as it had any, was to induce a peculiar concentration upon something visual, and to set in motion an expanding succession of concentric feelings. Some of Miss Moore's poems – for instance with animal or bird subjects – have a very wide spread of association. It would be difficult to say what is the 'subject-matter' of *The Jerboa*. For a mind of such agility, and for a sensibility so reticent, the minor subject, such as a pleasant little sand-coloured skipping animal, may be the best release for the major emotions. Only the pedantic literalist could consider the subject-matter to be trivial; the triviality is in himself. We all have to choose whatever subject-matter allows us the most powerful and most secret release; and that is a personal affair.

The result is often something that the majority will call frigid; for feeling in one's own way, however intensely, is likely to look like frigidity to those who can only feel in accepted ways.

> The deepest feeling always shows itself in silence;
> not in silence, but restraint.

It shows itself in a control which makes possible the fusion of the ironic-conversational and the high-rhetorical, as

> I recall their magnificence, now not more magnificent
> than it is dim. It is difficult to recall the ornament,
>   speech, and precise manner of what one might
>   call the minor acquaintances twenty
>   years back. . . .
>   strict with tension, malignant
>   in its power over us and deeper
>   than the sea when it proffers flattery in exchange
>   for hemp,
>   rye, flax, horses, platinum, timber and fur.

As one would expect from the kind of activity which I have been trying to indicate, Miss Moore's versification is anything but 'free'. Many of the poems are in exact, and sometimes complicated, formal patterns, and move with the elegance of a minuet. ('Elegance', indeed, is one of her certain attributes.) Some of the poems (e.g. *Marriage*, *An Octopus*) are unrhymed; in others (e.g. *Sea Unicorns and Land Unicorns*) rhyme or assonance is introduced irregularly; in a number of the poems rhyme is part of a regular pattern interwoven with unrhymed endings. Miss Moore's use of rhyme is in itself a definite innovation in metric.

In the conventional forms of rhyme the stress given by the rhyme tends to fall in the same place as the stress given by the sense. The extreme case, at its best, is the pentameter couplet of Pope. Poets before and after Pope have given variety, sometimes at the expense of smoothness, by deliberately separating the stresses, from time to time; but this separation – often effected simply by longer periods or more involved syntax – can hardly be considered as more than a deviation from the norm for the purpose of avoiding monotony. The tendency of some of the best contemporary poetry is of course to dispense with rhyme altogether; but some of those who do use it have used it here and there to make a pattern directly in contrast with the sense and rhythm pattern, to give a greater intricacy. Some of the internal rhyming of Hopkins is to the point. (Genuine or auditory internal rhyme must not be confused with false or visual internal rhyme. If a poem reads just as well when cut up so that all the rhymes fall at the end of lines, then the internal rhyme is false and only a typographical caprice, as in Oscar Wilde's *Sphinx*.) This rhyme, which forms a pattern *against* the metric and sense pattern of the poem, may be either heavy or light – that is to say, either *heavier* or *lighter* than the other pattern. The two kinds, heavy and light, have doubtless different uses which remain to be explored. Of the *light* rhyme Miss

Moore is the greatest living master; and indeed she is the first, so far as I know, who has investigated its possibilities. It will be observed that the effect sometimes requires giving a word a slightly more analytical pronunciation, or stressing a syllable more than ordinarily:

al-

ways has been—at the antipodes from the init-
   ial great truths. 'Part of it was crawling, part of it
was about to crawl, the rest
   was torpid in its lair.' In the short-legged, fit-
ful advance. . . .

It is sometimes obtained by the use of articles as rhyme words:

an
injured fan.
   The barnacles which encrust the side
   of the wave, cannot hide . . .

the
turquoise sea
   of bodies. The water drives a wedge . . .

In a good deal of what is sometimes (with an unconscious theological innuendo) called 'modernist' verse one finds either an excess or a defect of technical attention. The former appears in an emphasis upon words rather than things, and the latter in an emphasis upon things and an indifference to words. In either case, the poem is formless, just as the most accomplished sonnet, if it is an attempt to express matter unsuitable for sonnet form, is formless. But a precise fitness of form and matter means also a balance between them: thus the form, the pattern movement, has a solemnity of its own (e.g. Shakespeare's songs), however light and gay the human emotion concerned; and a gaiety of its own, however serious or tragic the emotion. The choruses of Sophocles, as well as the songs of Shakespeare, have another concern besides the human action of which they are spectators, and without this other concern there is not poetry. And on the other hand, if you aim only at the poetry in poetry, there is no poetry either.

My conviction, for what it is worth, has remained unchanged for the last fourteen years: that Miss Moore's poems form part of the small body of durable poetry written in our time; of that small body of writings, among what passes for poetry, in which an original sensibility and alert intelligence and deep feeling have been engaged in maintaining the life of the English language.

The original suggestion was that I should make a selection, from both previously published and more recent poems. But Miss Moore exercised her own rights of proscription first, so drastically, that I have been concerned to preserve rather than abate. I have therefore hardly done more than settle the order of the contents. This book contains all that Miss Moore was willing to reprint from the volume *Observations* (The Dial Press, New York, 1924), together with the poems written since that date which she is willing to publish.

T.S.E.
August, 1934

Contents

Certain of these poems first appeared in *Poetry*, *The Hound and Horn*, and *The Criterion*.

SELECTED POEMS

Part of a Novel, Part of a Poem, Part of a Play

THE STEEPLE-JACK

Dürer would have seen a reason for living
    in a town like this, with eight stranded whales
to look at; with the sweet sea air coming into your house
on a fine day, from water etched
    with waves as formal as the scales
on a fish.

One by one, in two's, in three's, the seagulls keep
    flying back and forth over the town clock,
or sailing around the lighthouse without moving the wings—
rising steadily with a slight
    quiver of the body—or flock
mewing where

a sea the purple of the peacock's neck is
    paled to greenish azure as Dürer changed
the pine green of the Tyrol to peacock blue and guinea
grey. You can see a twenty-five-
    pound lobster; and fishnets arranged
to dry. The

whirlwind fife-and-drum of the storm bends the salt
    marsh grass, disturbs stars in the sky and the
star on the steeple; it is a privilege to see so
much confusion. Disguised by what
    might seem austerity, the sea-
side flowers and

trees are favoured by the fog so that you have
     the tropics at first hand: the trumpet-vine,
fox-glove, giant snap-dragon, a salpiglossis that has
spots and stripes; morning-glories, gourds,
     or moon-vines trained on fishing-twine
at the back

door. There are no banyans, frangipani, nor
     jack-fruit trees; nor an exotic serpent
life. Ring lizard and snake-skin for the foot, or crocodile;
but here they've cats, not cobras, to
     keep down the rats. The diffident
little newt

with white pin-dots on black horizontal spaced
     out bands lives here; yet there is nothing that
ambition can buy or take away. The college student
named Ambrose sits on the hill-side
     with his not-native books and hat
and sees boats

at sea progress white and rigid as if in
     a groove. Liking an elegance of which
the source is not bravado, he knows by heart the antique
sugar-bowl-shaped summer-house of
     interlacing slats, and the pitch
of the church

spire, not true, from which a man in scarlet lets
     down a rope as a spider spins a thread;
he might be part of a novel, but on the sidewalk a
sign says C. J. Poole, Steeple Jack,
     in black and white; and one in red
and white says

Danger. The church portico has four fluted
    columns, each a single piece of stone, made
modester by white-wash. This would be a fit haven for
waifs, children, animals, prisoners,
    and presidents who have repaid
sin-driven

senators by not thinking about them. There
    are a school-house, a post-office in a
store, fish-houses, hen-houses, a three-masted schooner on
the stocks. The hero, the student,
    the steeple-jack, each in his way,
is at home.

It could not be dangerous to be living
    in a town like this, of simple people,
who have a steeple-jack placing danger signs by the church
while he is gilding the solid-
    pointed star, which on a steeple
stands for hope.

THE HERO

Where there is personal liking we go.
    Where the ground is sour; where there are
    weeds of beanstalk height,
    snakes' hypodermic teeth, or
    the wind brings the 'scarebabe voice'
    from the neglected yew set with
    the semi-precious cat's eyes of the owl—
awake, asleep, 'raised ears extended to fine points', and so
on—love won't grow.

We do not like some things, and the hero
   doesn't; deviating head-stones
   and uncertainty;
   going where one does not wish
   to go; suffering and not
   saying so; standing and listening where something
   is hiding. The hero shrinks
as what it is flies out on muffled wings, with twin yellow
eyes—to and fro—

with quavering water-whistle note, low,
   high, in basso-falsetto chirps
   until the skin creeps.
   Jacob when a-dying, asked
   Joseph: Who are these? and blessed
   both sons, the younger most, vexing Joseph. And
   Joseph was vexing to some.
Cincinnatus was; Regulus; and some of our fellow
men have been, though

devout, like Pilgrim having to go slow
   to find his roll; tired but hopeful—
   hope not being hope
   until all ground for hope has
   vanished; and lenient, looking
   upon a fellow creature's error with the
   feelings of a mother—a
woman or a cat. The decorous frock-coated Negro
by the grotto

answers the fearless sightseeing hobo
   who asks the man she's with, what's this,
   what's that, where's Martha
   buried, 'Gen-ral Washington

there; his lady, here'; speaking
as if in a play—not seeing her; with a
sense of human dignity
and reverence for mystery, standing like the shadow
of the willow.

Moses would not be grandson to Pharaoh.
It is not what I eat that is
my natural meat,
the hero says.   He's not out
seeing a sight but the rock
crystal thing to see—the startling El Greco
brimming with inner light—that
covets nothing that it has let go. This then you may know
as the hero.

The Jerboa

A Roman hired an
artist, a freedman,
   to make a cone—pine-cone
   or fir-cone—with holes for a fountain. Placed on
     the Prison of St Angelo, this cone
     of the Pompeys which is known

now as the Popes', passed
for art. A huge cast
   bronze, dwarfing the peacock
   statue in the garden of the Vatican,
     it looks like a work of art made to give
     to a Pompey, or native

of Thebes.   Others could
build, and understood
   making colossi and
   how to use slaves, and kept crocodiles and put
     baboons on the necks of giraffes to pick
     fruit, and used serpent magic.

They had their men tie
hippopotami
   and bring out dapple dog-
   cats to course antelopes, dikdik, and ibex;
     or used small eagles. They looked on as theirs,
     impallas and onigers,

the wild ostrich herd
with hard feet and bird
    necks rearing back in the
    dust like a serpent preparing to strike, cranes,
        storks, anoas, mongooses, and Nile geese.
        And there were gardens for these—

combining planes, dates,
limes, and pomegranates,
    in avenues—with square
    pools of pink flowers, tame fish, and small frogs. Besides
        yarns dyed with indigo, and red cotton,
        they had a flax which they spun

into fine linen
cordage for yachtsmen.
    These people liked small things;
    they gave to boys little paired playthings such as
        nests of eggs, ichneumon and snake, paddle
        and raft, badger and camel;

and made toys for them-
selves: the royal totem;
    and toilet-boxes marked
    with the contents. Lords and ladies put goose-grease
        paint in round bone boxes with pivoting
        lid incised with the duck-wing

or reverted duck-
head; kept in a buck
    or rhinoceros horn,
    the ground horn; and locust oil in stone locusts.
        It was a picture with a fine distance;
        of drought, and of assistance

in time, from the Nile
rising slowly, while
   the pig-tailed monkey on
   slab-hands, with arched-up slack-slung gait, and the brown
      dandy, looked at the jasmine two-leafed twig
      and bud, cactus-pads, and fig.

Dwarfs here and there, lent
to an evident
   poetry of frog grays,
   duck-egg greens, and egg-plant blues, a fantasy
      and a verisimilitude that were
      right to those with, everywhere,

power over the poor.
The bees' food is your
   food. Those who tended flower-
   beds and stables were like the king's cane in the
      form of a hand, or the folding bedroom
      made for his mother of whom

he was fond. Princes
clad in queens' dresses
   calla or petunia
   white that trembled at the edge, and queens in a
      king's underskirt of fine-twilled thread like silk-
      worm gut, as bee-man and milk-

maid, kept divine cows
and bees; limestone brows,
   and gold-foil wings. They made
   basalt serpents and portraits of beetles; the
      king gave his name to them and he was named
      for them. He feared snakes and tamed

Pharaoh's rat, the rust-
backed mongoose. No bust
   of it was made, but there
   was pleasure for the rat. Its restlessness was
      its excellence; it was praised for its wit;
      and the jerboa, like it,

a small desert rat,
and not famous, that
   lives without water, has
   happiness. Abroad seeking food, or at home
      in its burrow, the Sahara field-mouse
      has a shining silver house

of sand. O rest and
joy, the boundless sand,
   the stupendous sand-spout,
   no water, no palm-trees, no ivory bed,
      tiny cactus; but one would not be he
      who has nothing but plenty.

ABUNDANCE

Africanus meant
the conqueror sent
   from Rome.   It should mean the
   untouched: the sand-brown jumping-rat—free-born; and
      the blacks, that choice race with an elegance
      ignored by one's ignorance.

Part terrestrial,
and part celestial,
   Jacob saw, cudgel staff
   in claw-hand—steps of air and air angels; his

friends were the stones. The translucent mistake
of the desert, does not make

hardship for one who
can rest and then do
   the opposite—launching
   as if on wings, from its match-thin hind legs, in
      daytime or at night; that departs with great
      speed, followed by, as a weight,

a double length, thin
tail furred like the skin;
   that curls round it when it
   sleeps 'round'—the nose nested in fur, a hind leg
      at each side of the head—or lies lengthwise,
      in view, when the body lies

flat. Seen by daylight,
the body is white
   in front; and on the back,
   buffy-brown like the breast of the fawn-breasted
      bower-bird. It hops like the fawn-breast, but has
      chipmunk contours—perceived as

it turns its bird head—
the nap directed
   neatly back and blending
   with the ear which reiterates the slimness
      of the body. The fine hairs on the tail,
      repeating the other pale

markings, lengthen till
at the tip they fill
   out in a tuft—black and

white; strange detail of the simplified creature,
   fish-shaped and silvered to steel by the force
   of the large desert moon. Course

the jerboa, or
plunder its food store,
   and you will be cursed. It
   honours the sand by assuming its colour;
      closed upper paws seeming one with the fur
      in its flight from a danger.

By fifths and sevenths,
in leaps of two lengths,
   like the uneven notes
   of the Bedouin flute, it stops its gleaning
      on little wheel castors, and makes fern-seed
      foot-prints with kangaroo speed.

Its leaps should be set
to the flageolet;
   pillar body erect
   on a three-cornered smooth-working Chippendale
      claw—propped on hind legs, and tail as third toe,
      between leaps to its burrow.

Camellia Sabina

and the Bordeaux plum
from Marmande (France in parentheses) with
A. G. on the base of the jar—Alexis Godillot—
unevenly blown beside a bubble that
is green when held up to the light; they
are a fine duet; the screw-top for this graft-grown
   briar-black bloom on black-thorn pigeon's-blood
   is, like Certosa, sealed with foil. Appropriate custom.

And they keep under
glass also, camellias catalogued by
lines across the leaf. The French are a cruel race—willing
to squeeze the diner's cucumber or broil a
meal on vine-shoots. Gloria mundi
with a leaf two inches, nine lines broad, they have; and
   the smaller, Camellia Sabina
   with amanita-white petals; there are several of her

pale pinwheels, and pale
stripe that looks as if on a mushroom the
sliver from a beet-root carved into a rose were laid. 'Dry
the windows with a cloth fastened to a staff.
In the camellia-house there must be
no smoke from the stove, nor dew on the windows, lest
   the plants ail,' the amateur is told;
   'mistakes are irreparable and nothing will avail.'

The scentless nosegay
is thus formed in the midst of the bouquet
from bottles casks and corks for: sixty-four million red wines

and twenty million white, which Bordeaux merchants
and lawyers 'have spent a great deal of
trouble' to select, from what was and what was not
   Bordeaux. A food-grape, however—'born
   of nature and of art'—is true ground for the grape-holiday.

    The food of a wild
   mouse in some countries is wild parsnip- or sunflower- or
   morning-glory-seed, with an occasional
   grape. Underneath the vines of the Bolzano
   grape of Italy, the Prince of Tails
   might stroll. Does yonder mouse with a grape in its hand
     and its child in its mouth, not portray
     the Spanish fleece suspended by the neck? In that well-
       piled

 larder above your
head, the picture of what you will eat is
looked at from the end of the avenue. The wire cage is
locked, but by bending down and studying the
roof, it is possible to see the
pantomime of Persian thought: the gilded, too tight,
   undemure coat of gems unruined
   by the rain—each small pebble of jade that refused to
     mature,

    plucked delicately
   off. Off jewelry not meant to keep Tom
   Thumb, the cavalry cadet, on his Italian upland
   meadow-mouse, from looking at the grapes beneath
   the interrupted light from them, and
   dashing round the *concours hippique* of the tent, in
     a flurry of eels, scallops, serpents,
     and other shadows from the blue of the green canopy.

The wine-cellar? No.
It accomplishes nothing and makes the
soul heavy. The gleaning is more than the vintage, though the
history *de la vigne et du vin* place a
mirabelle in the *bibliothèque*
unique depuis seventeen-ninety-seven. (Close
   the window, says the Abbé Berlèse,
      for Sabina born under glass.) O generous Bolzano!

No Swan So Fine

'No water so still as the
     dead fountains of Versailles.' No swan,
with swart blind look askance
and gondoliering legs, so fine
     as the chintz china one with fawn-
brown eyes and toothed gold
collar on to show whose bird it was.

Lodged in the Louis Fifteenth
     candelabrum-tree of cockscomb-
tinted buttons, dahlias,
sea-urchins, and everlastings,
     it perches on the branching foam
of polished sculptured
flowers—at ease and tall. The king is dead.

The Plumet Basilisk

In blazing driftwood
   the green keeps showing at the same place;
as, intermittently, the fire-opal shows blue and green.
   In Costa Rica the true Chinese lizard face
is found, of the amphibious falling dragon, the living firework.

He leaps and meets his
   likeness in the stream and, king with king,
helped by his three-part plume along the back, runs on two legs,
   tail dragging; faints upon the air; then with a spring
dives to the stream-bed, hiding as the chieftain with gold body
       hid in

Guatavita Lake.
   He runs, he flies, he swims, to get to
his basilica—'the ruler of Rivers, Lakes, and Seas,
   invisible or visible', with clouds to do
as bid—and can be 'long or short, and also coarse or fine at
       pleasure'.

THE MALAY DRAGON

We have ours; and they
   have theirs. Ours has a skin feather crest;
theirs has wings out from the waist which is snuff-brown or
       sallow.
   Ours falls from trees on water; theirs is the smallest
dragon that knows how to dive head-first from a tree-top to
       something dry.

Floating on spread ribs,
    the boat-like body settles on the
clamshell-tinted spray sprung from the nutmeg-tree—minute
            legs
    trailing half akimbo—the true divinity
of Malay. Among unfragrant orchids, on the unnutritious nut

tree, *myristica*
    fragrans, the harmless god spreads ribs that
do not raise a hood. This is the serpent-dove peculiar
    to the East; that lives as the butterfly or bat
can, in a brood, conferring wings on what it grasps, as the air-
            plant does.

THE TUATERA

Elsewhere, sea lizards—
    congregated so there is not room
to step, with tails laid criss-cross, alligator-style, among
    birds toddling in and out—are innocent of whom
they neighbour. Bird-reptile social life is pleasing. The tuatera

will tolerate a
    petrel in its den, and lays ten eggs
or nine—the number laid by dragons since 'a true dragon
    has nine sons'. The frilled lizard, the kind with no legs,
and the three-horned chameleon, are non-serious ones that take
            to flight

if you do not. In
    Copenhagen the principal door
of the bourse is roofed by two pairs of dragons standing on
    their heads—twirled by the architect—so that the four
green tails conspiring upright, symbolize four-fold security.
        Now,

where sapotans drop
   their nuts out on the stream, there is, as
I have said, one of the quickest lizards in the world—the
   basilisk—that feeds on leaves and berries and has
shade from palm-vines, ferns, and peperomias; or lies basking
      on a

horizontal branch
   from which sour-grass and orchids sprout. If
best, he lets go, smites the water, and runs on it—a thing
   difficult for fingered feet. But when captured—stiff
and somewhat heavy, like fresh putty on the hand—he is no
      longer

the slight lizard that
   can stand in a receding flattened
S—small, long and vertically serpentine or, sagging,
   span the bushes in a fox's bridge. Vines suspend
the weight of something's shadow fixed on silk. By the Chinese
      brush, eight green

bands are painted on
   the tail—as piano keys are barred
by five black stripes across the white. This octave of faulty
   decorum hides the extraordinary lizard
till night-fall, which is for man the basilisk whose look will kill;
      but is

for lizards men can
   kill, the welcome dark—with the galloped
ground-bass of the military drum, the squeak of bag-pipes
   and of bats. Hollow whistled monkey-notes disrupt
the castanets. Taps from the back of the bow sound odd on last
      year's gourd,

or when they touch the
    kettledrums—at which, for there's no light,
a scared frog screaming like a bird, leaps out from weeds in
        which
    it could have hid, with curves of the meteorite,
the curve of whose diving no diver refutes. Upon spider-hands,
        with

                wide water-bug strokes,
            in jerks which express
            a regal and excellent awkwardness,

            the plumet portrays
            mythology's wish
            to be interchangeably man and fish—

        travelling rapidly upward, as
        spider-clawed fingers can twang the
        bass strings of the harp, and with steps
        as articulate, make their way
        back to retirement on strings that
        vibrate till the claws are spread flat.

            Among tightened wires,
            minute noises swell
            and change as in the woods' acoustic shell

            they will, with trees as
            avenues of steel
            to veil invisibleness ears must feel—

        black opal emerald opal
        emerald—the prompt-delayed loud-
        low chromatic listened-for down-

scale which Swinburne called in prose, the
noiseless music that hangs about
the serpent when it stirs or springs.

No anonymous
nightingale sings in a swamp, fed on
sound from porcupine-quilled palm-trees blurring at the edge,
that
rattle like the rain. This is our Tower-of-London
jewel that the Spaniards failed to see, among the feather capes
and hawk's-

head moths and black-chinned
humming-birds; the innocent, rare, gold-
defending dragon that as you look begins to be a
nervous naked sword on little feet, with three-fold
separate flame above the hilt, inhabiting fringe equidistant

from itself, of white
fire eating into air. Thus nested
in the phosphorescent alligator that copies each
digression of the shape, he pants and settles—head
up and eyes black as the molested bird's, with look of whetted
fierceness,

in what is merely
breathing and recoiling from the hand.
Thinking himself hid among the yet unfound jade axeheads,
silver jaguars and bats, and amethysts and
polished iron, gold in a ten-ton chain, and pearls the size of
pigeon-eggs,

he is alive there
in his basilisk cocoon beneath

the one of living green; his quicksilver ferocity
    quenched in the rustle of his fall into the sheath
which is the shattering sudden splash that marks his temporary
        loss.

The Frigate Pelican

Rapidly cruising or lying on the air there is a bird
    that realizes Rasselas's friend's project
    of wings uniting levity with strength. This
        hell-diver, frigate-bird, hurricane-
bird; unless swift is the proper word
      for him, the storm omen when
    he flies close to the waves, should be seen
        fishing, although oftener
        he appears to prefer

to take, on the wing, from industrious cruder-winged species
    the fish they have caught, and is seldom successless.
    A marvel of grace, no matter how fast his
        victim may fly or how often may
turn, the dishonest pelican's ease
      in pursuit, bears him away
    with the fish that the badgered bird drops.
        A kind of superlative
        swallow, that likes to live

on food caught while flying, he is not a pelican. The toe
    with slight web, air-boned body, and very long wings
    with the spread of a swan's—duplicating a
        bow-string as he floats overhead—feel
the changing V-shaped scissor swallow-
      tail direct the rigid keel.
    And steering beak to windward always,
        the fleetest foremost fairy
        among birds, outflies the

aeroplane which cannot flap its wings nor alter any quill-
    tip. For him, the feeling in a hand, in fins, is
    in his unbent downbent crafty oar.   With him
        other pelicans aimlessly soar
as he does; separating, until
        not flapping they rise once more,
    closing in without looking and move
            outward again to the top
            of the circle and stop

and blow back, allowing the wind to reverse their direction.
    This is not the stalwart swan that can ferry the
    woodcutter's two children home; no. Make hay; keep
        the shop; I have one sheep; were a less
limber animal's mottoes. This one
        finds sticks for the swan's-down dress
    of his child to rest upon and would
            not know Gretel from Hänsel.
            As impassioned Handel—

meant for a lawyer and a masculine German domestic
    career—clandestinely studied the harpsichord
    and never was known to have fallen in love,
        the unconfiding frigate-bird hides
in the height and in the majestic
        display of his art. He glides
    a hundred feet or quivers about
            as charred paper behaves—full
            of feints; and an eagle

of vigilance, earns the term aquiline; keeping at a height
    so great the feathers look black and the beak does not
    show. It is not retreat but exclusion from
        which he looks down and observes what went

secretly, as it thought, out of sight
among dense jungle plants. Sent
ahead of the rest, there goes the true
knight in his jointed coat that
covers all but his bat

ears; a-trot, with stiff pig gait—our tame armadillo, loosed by
his master and as pleased as a dog. Beside the
spattered blood—that orchid which the native fears—
the fer-de-lance lies sleeping; centaur-
like, this harmful couple's amity
is apropos. A jaguar
and crocodile are fighting. Sharp-shinned
hawks and peacock-freckled small
cats, like the literal

merry-go-round, come wandering within the circular view
of the high bird for whom from the air they are ants
keeping house all their lives in the crack of a
crag with no view from the top. And here,
unlikely animals learning to
dance, crouch on two steeds that rear
behind a leopard with a frantic
face, tamed by an Artemis
who wears a dress like his,

and hampering haymaker's hat. *Festina lente*. Be gay
civilly. How so? 'If I do well I am blessed
whether any bless me or not, and if I do
ill I am cursed.' We watch the moon rise
on the Susquehanna. In his way
this most romantic bird, flies
to a more mundane place, the mangrove
swamp, to sleep.   He wastes the moon.
But he, and others, soon

rise from the bough, and though flying are able to foil the tired
   moment of danger, that lays on heart and lungs the
   weight of the python that crushes to powder.
      The tune's illiterate footsteps fail;
the steam hacks are not to be admired.
      These, unturbulent, avail
   themselves of turbulence to fly—pleased
         with the faint wind's varyings,
         on which to spread fixed wings.

The reticent lugubrious ragged immense minuet
   descending to leeward, ascending to windward
   again without flapping, in what seems to be
      a way of resting, are now nearer,
but as seemingly bodiless yet
      as they were.   Theirs are sombre
   quills for so wide and lightboned a bird
         as the frigate pelican
         of the Caribbean.

The Buffalo

Black in blazonry means
prudence; and niger, unpropitious. Might
hematite-
   black incurved compact horns on a bison
      have significance? The
   soot brown tail-tuft on
      a kind of lion-

tail; what would that express?
And John Steuart Curry's Ajax pulling
grass—no ring
   in his nose—two birds standing on his back?
      though prints like this cannot
   show if they were black
      birds, nor the colour

of the back. The modern
ox does not look like the Augsburg ox's
portrait. Yes,
   the great extinct wild Aurochs was a beast
      to paint, with stripe and six-
   foot horn-spread—decreased
      to Siamese-cat-

Brown Swiss size, or zebu
shape with white plush dewlap and warm-blooded
hump; to red-
   skinned Hereford or to piebald Holstein. Yet
      some would say the sparse-haired
   buffalo has met
      human notions best—

      unlike the elephant,
both jewel and jeweller in the hairs
that he wears—
   no white-nosed Vermont ox yoked with its twin
     to haul the maple sap,
   up to their knees in
      snow; no freakishly

      Over-Drove Ox drawn by
Rowlandson, but the Indian buffalo,
albino-
   footed, standing in the mud-lake, with a
     day's work to do. No white
   Christian heathen, way-
      laid by the Buddha,

     serves him so well as the
buffalo—as mettlesome as if check-
reined—free neck
   stretching out, and snake-tail in a half twist
     on the flank; nor will so
   cheerfully assist
      the Sage sitting with

     feet at the same side, to
dismount at the shrine; nor are there any
ivory
   tusks like those two horns which when a tiger
     coughs, are lowered fiercely
   and convert the fur
      to harmless rubbish.

     The Indian buffalo,
led by bare-leggèd herd-boys to a hay

hut where they
    stable it, need not fear comparison
        with bison, with the twins,
    nor with anyone
            of ox ancestry.

Nine Nectarines and Other Porcelain

Arranged by two's as peaches are,
at intervals that all may live—
eight and a single one, on twigs that
grew the year before—they look like
a derivative;
although not uncommonly
the opposite is seen—
nine peaches on a nectarine.
Fuzzless through slender crescent leaves
of green or blue—or both,
in the Chinese style—the four

pairs' half-moon leaf-mosaic turns
out to the sun the sprinkled blush
of puce-American-Beauty pink
applied to beeswax gray by the
unenquiring brush
of mercantile bookbinding.
Like the peach *Yu*, the red-
cheeked peach which cannot aid the dead,
but eaten in time prevents death,
the Italian peach-
nut, Persian plum, Ispahan

secluded wall-grown nectarine,
as wild spontaneous fruit was
found in China first. But was it wild?
Prudent de Candolle would not say.
We cannot find flaws
in this emblematic group

of nine, with leaf window
unquilted by curculio—
    which someone once depicted on
        this much-mended plate; or
        in the also accurate

    unantlered moose, or Iceland horse,
or ass, asleep against the old
    thick, low-leaning nectarine that is the
    colour of the shrub-tree's brownish
flower. From manifold
    small boughs, productive as the
magic willow that grew
above the mother's grave and threw
    on Cinderella what she wished,
        a bat is winging. It
        is a moonlight scene, bringing

    the animal so near, its eyes
are separate from the face—mere
    delicately drawn gray discs, out from
    itself in space. Imperial
happiness lives here
    on the peaches of long life
that make it permanent.
A fungus could have meant
    long life; a crane, a stork, a dove.
        China, with flowers and birds
        and half-beasts, became the land

    of the best china-making first.
Hunts and domestic scenes occur
    in France on dinner-plates, signed on the
    back with a two-finned fish; England

has an officer
in jack-boots seated in a
bosquet, the cow, the flock
of sheep, the pheasant, the peacock
sweeping near with lifted claw; the
skilled peonian rose
and the rosebud that began

with William Billingsley (once poor,
like a monkey on a dolphin, tossed
by Ocean, mighty monster) until
Josiah Spode adopted him.
Yet with the gold-glossed
serpent handles, are there green
cocks with 'brown beaks and cheeks
and dark blue combs' and mammal freaks
that, like the Chinese Certainties
and sets of Precious Things,
dare to be conspicuous?

Theirs is a race that 'understands
the spirit of the wilderness'
and the nectarine-loving kylin
of pony appearance—the long-
tailed or the tailless
small cinnamon-brown common
camel-haired unicorn
with antelope feet and no horn,
here enamelled on porcelain.
It was a Chinese who
imagined this masterpiece.

The Fish

wade
through black jade.
   Of the crow-blue mussel-shells, one keeps
   adjusting the ash heaps;
     opening and shutting itself like

an
injured fan.
   The barnacles which encrust the side
   of the wave, cannot hide
     there for the submerged shafts of the

sun,
split like spun
   glass, move themselves with spotlight swiftness
   into the crevices—
     in and out, illuminating

the
turquoise sea
   of bodies. The water drives a wedge
   of iron through the iron edge
     of the cliff, whereupon the stars,

pink
rice grains, ink
   bespattered jelly-fish, crabs like green
   lilies and submarine
     toadstools, slide each on the other.

All
external
   marks of abuse are present on this
   defiant edifice—
      all the physical features of

ac-
cident—lack
   of cornice, dynamite grooves, burns, and
   hatchet strokes, these things stand
      out on it; the chasm-side is

dead.
Repeated
   evidence has proved that it can live
   on what cannot revive
      its youth. The sea grows old in it.

In This Age of Hard Trying, Nonchalance is Good and

'really, it is not the
    business of the gods to bake clay pots'. They did not
      do it in this instance. A few
        revolved upon the axes of their worth
    as if excessive popularity might be a pot;

they did not venture the
    profession of humility. The polished wedge
      that might have split the firmament
        was dumb. At last it threw itself away
    and falling down, conferred on some poor fool, a privilege.

'Taller by the length of
    a conversation of five hundred years than all
      the others,' there was one, whose tales
        of what could never have been actual—
    were better than the haggish, uncompanionable drawl

of certitude; his by-
    play was more terrible in its effectiveness
      than the fiercest frontal attack.
        The staff, the bag, the feigned inconsequence
    of manner, best bespeak that weapon, self protectiveness.

To Statecraft Embalmed

There is nothing to be said for you. Guard
Your secret. Conceal it under your hard
  Plumage, necromancer.
     O
Bird, whose tents were 'awnings of Egyptian
Yarn', shall Justice' faint, zigzag inscription—
  Leaning like a dancer—
     Show
The pulse of its once vivid sovereignty?
You say not, and transmigrating from the
  Sarcophagus, you wind
     Snow
Silence round us and with moribund talk,
Half limping and half-ladyfied, you stalk
  About. Ibis, we find
     No
Virtue in you—alive and yet so dumb.
Discreet behaviour is not now the sum
  Of statesmanlike good sense.
     Though
It were the incarnation of dead grace?
As if a death-mask ever could replace
  Life's faulty excellence!
     Slow
To remark the steep, too strict proportion
Of your throne, you'll see the wrenched distortion
  Of suicidal dreams
     Go
Staggering toward itself and with its bill

Attack its own identity, until
　　Foe seems friend and friend seems
　　　Foe.

Poetry

I too, dislike it: there are things that are important beyond all
        this fiddle.
  Reading it, however, with a perfect contempt for it, one dis-
        covers in
  it after all, a place for the genuine.
    Hands that can grasp, eyes
    that can dilate, hair that can rise
      if it must, these things are important not because a

high-sounding interpretation can be put upon them but because
        they are
  useful. When they become so derivative as to become un-
        intelligible,
  the same thing may be said for all of us, that we
    do not admire what
    we cannot understand: the bat,
      holding on upside down or in quest of something to

eat, elephants pushing, a wild horse taking a roll, a tireless wolf
        under
  a tree, the immovable critic twitching his skin like a horse
        that feels a flea, the base-
  ball fan, the statistician—
    nor is it valid
      to discriminate against 'business documents and

school-books'; all these phenomena are important. One must
        make a distinction
  however: when dragged into prominence by half poets, the
        result is not poetry,

nor till the poets among us can be
  'literalists of
  the imagination'—above
    insolence and triviality and can present

for inspection, imaginary gardens with real toads in them, shall
      we have
  it. In the meantime, if you demand on one hand,
  the raw material of poetry in
    all its rawness and
    that which is on the other hand
      genuine, then you are interested in poetry.

Pedantic Literalist

Prince Rupert's drop, paper muslin ghost,
    White torch—'with power to say unkind
Things with kindness, and the most
        Irritating things in the midst of love and
            Tears', you invite destruction.

You are like the meditative man
    With the perfunctory heart; its
Carved cordiality ran
        To and fro at first like an inlaid and royal
            Immutable production;

Then afterward 'neglected to be
    Painful, deluding him with
Loitering formality',
        'Doing its duty as if it did it not',
            Presenting an obstruction

To the motive that it served. What stood
    Erect in you has withered. A
Little 'palm-tree of turned wood'
        Informs your once spontaneous core in its
            Immutable production.

Critics and Connoisseurs

There is a great amount of poetry in unconscious
    fastidiousness. Certain Ming
        products, imperial floor-coverings of coach-
    wheel yellow, are well enough in their way but I have seen
                something
        that I like better—a
            mere childish attempt to make an imperfectly bal-
                lasted animal stand up,
            similar determination to make a pup
                eat his meat from the plate.

I remember a swan under the willows in Oxford,
    with flamingo-coloured, maple-
        leaflike feet. It reconnoitred like a battle-
    ship. Disbelief and conscious fastidiousness were the staple
            ingredients in its
                disinclination to move. Finally its hardihood was not
                    proof against its
                proclivity to more fully appraise such bits
                of food as the stream

bore counter to it; it made away with what I gave it
    to eat. I have seen this swan and
        I have seen you; I have seen ambition without
    understanding in a variety of forms. Happening to stand
            by an ant-hill, I have
                seen a fastidious ant carrying a stick north, south,
                    east, west, till it turned on
                itself, struck out from the flower-bed into the lawn,
                    and returned to the point

from which it had started. Then abandoning the stick as
    useless and overtaxing its
        jaws with a particle of whitewash—pill-like but
    heavy, it again went through the same course of procedure.
                What is
            there in being able
                to say that one has dominated the stream in an
                    attitude of self-defence;
                in proving that one has had the experience
                    of carrying a stick?

The Monkeys

winked too much and were afraid of snakes. The zebras,
        supreme in
their abnormality; the elephants with their fog-coloured skin
  and strictly practical appendages
     were there, the small cats; and the parakeet—
       trivial and humdrum on examination, destroying
     bark and portions of the food it could not eat.

I recall their magnificence, now not more magnificent
than it is dim. It is difficult to recall the ornament,
  speech, and precise manner of what one might
     call the minor acquaintances twenty
       years back; but I shall not forget him—that Gilgamesh
        among
     the hairy carnivora—that cat with the

wedge-shaped, slate-gray marks on its forelegs and the resolute
        tail,
astringently remarking, 'They have imposed on us with their
        pale
  half-fledged protestations, trembling about
     in inarticulate frenzy, saying
       it is not for us to understand art; finding it
     all so difficult, examining the thing

as if it were inconceivably arcanic, as symmet-
rically frigid as if it had been carved out of chrysoprase
  or marble—strict with tension, malignant
     in its power over us and deeper
       than the sea when it proffers flattery in exchange for
        hemp,
     rye, flax, horses, platinum, timber, and fur.'

Roses Only

You do not seem to realize that beauty is a liability rather than
    an asset—that in view of the fact that spirit creates form we
        are justified in supposing
        that you must have brains. For you, a symbol of the unit,
            stiff and sharp,
    conscious of surpassing by dint of native superiority and lik-
        ing for everything
self-dependent, anything an

ambitious civilization might produce: for you, unaided, to
        attempt through sheer
    reserve, to confute presumptions resulting from observation,
        is idle. You cannot make us
        think you a delightful happen-so. But rose, if you are bril-
            liant, it
    is not because your petals are the without-which-nothing of
        pre-eminence. Would you not, minus
thorns, be a what-is-this, a mere

peculiarity? They are not proof against a worm, the elements,
        or mildew;
    but what about the predatory hand? What is brilliance with-
        out co-ordination? Guarding the
        infinitesimal pieces of your mind, compelling audience to
    the remark that it is better to be forgotten than to be remem-
            bered too violently,
your thorns are the best part of you.

Black Earth

Openly, yes,
with the naturalness
    of the hippopotamus or the alligator
    when it climbs out on the bank to experience the

sun, I do these
things which I do, which please
    no one but myself. Now I breathe and now I am sub-
    merged; the blemishes stand up and shout when the object

in view was a
renaissance; shall I say
    the contrary? The sediment of the river which
    encrusts my joints, makes me very gray but I am used

to it, it may
remain there; do away
    with it and I am myself done away with, for the
    patina of circumstance can but enrich what was

there to begin
with. This elephant-skin
    which I inhabit, fibred over like the shell of
    the cocoanut, this piece of black glass through which no
            light

can filter—cut
into checkers by rut
    upon rut of unpreventable experience—
    it is a manual for the peanut-tongued and the

hairy-toed. Black
but beautiful, my back
    is full of the history of power. Of power? What
    is powerful and what is not? My soul shall never

be cut into
by a wooden spear; through-
    out childhood to the present time, the unity of
    life and death has been expressed by the circumference

described by my
trunk; nevertheless, I
    perceive feats of strength to be inexplicable after
    all; and I am on my guard; external poise, it

has its centre
well nurtured—we know
    where—in pride; but spiritual poise, it has its centre where?
    My ears are sensitized to more than the sound of

the wind. I see
and I hear, unlike the
    wandlike body of which one hears so much, which was made
    to see and not to see; to hear and not to hear;

that tree-trunk without
roots, accustomed to shout
    its own thoughts to itself like a shell, maintained intact
    by one who knows what strange pressure of the
            atmosphere; that

spiritual
brother to the coral-
    plant, absorbed into which, the equable sapphire light
    becomes a nebulous green. The I of each is to

the I of each,
a kind of fretful speech
   which sets a limit on itself; the elephant is
   black earth preceded by a tendril? Compared with those

phenomena
which vacillate like a
   translucence of the atmosphere, the elephant is
   that on which darts cannot strike decisively the first

time, a substance
needful as an instance
   of the indestructibility of matter; it
   has looked at the electricity and at the earth-

quake and is still
here; the name means thick. Will
   depth be depth, thick skin be thick, to one who can see no
   beautiful element of unreason under it?

In the Days of Prismatic Colour

not in the days of Adam and Eve, but when Adam
    was alone; when there was no smoke and colour was
fine, not with the refinement
    of early civilization art, but because
of its originality; with nothing to modify it but the

mist that went up, obliqueness was a varia-
    tion of the perpendicular, plain to see and
to account for: it is no
    longer that; nor did the blue-red-yellow band
of incandescence that was colour keep its stripe: it also is one of

those things into which much that is peculiar can be
    read; complexity is not a crime but carry
it to the point of murki-
    ness and nothing is plain. Complexity,
moreover, that has been committed to darkness, instead of
        granting it-

self to be the pestilence that it is, moves all a-
    bout as if to bewilder us with the dismal
fallacy that insistence
    is the measure of achievement and that all
truth must be dark. Principally throat, sophistication is as it al-

ways has been—at the antipodes from the init-
    ial great truths. 'Part of it was crawling, part of it
was about to crawl, the rest
    was torpid in its lair.' In the short-legged, fit-
ful advance, the gurgling and all the minutiae—we have the
        classic

multitude of feet. To what purpose! Truth is no Apollo
   Belvedere, no formal thing. The wave may go over it if it
      likes.
Know that it will be there when it says,
   'I shall be there when the wave has gone by.'

Peter

Strong and slippery, built for the midnight grass-party con-
        fronted by four cats,
    he sleeps his time away—the detached first claw on his fore-
        leg, which corresponds
    to the thumb, retracted to its tip; the small tuft of fronds
      or katydid legs above each eye, still numbering the units in
        each group;
        the shadbones regularly set about his mouth, to droop
        or rise

in unison like the porcupine's quills—motionless. He lets him-
        self be flat-
    tened out by gravity, as it were a piece of seaweed tamed and
        weakened by
    exposure to the sun; compelled when extended, to lie
      stationary. Sleep is the result of his delusion that one must
        do as
        well as one can for oneself; sleep—epitome of what is to

him as to the average person, the end of life. Demonstrate on
        him how
    the lady caught the dangerous southern snake, placing a
        forked stick on either
    side of its innocuous neck; one need not try to stir
      him up; his prune-shaped head and alligator eyes are not a
        party to the
        joke. Lifted and handled, he may be dangled like an eel
        or set

up on the forearm like a mouse; his eyes bisected by pupils of a
        pin's

width, are flickeringly exhibited, then covered up. May be?
I should say,
might have been; when he has been got the better of in a
dream—as in a fight with nature or with cats—we all know
it. Profound sleep is
not with him a fixed illusion. Springing about with
froglike ac-

curacy, emitting jerky cries when taken in the hand, he is him-
self
again; to sit caged by the rungs of a domestic chair would be
unprofit-
able—human. What is the good of hypocrisy? It
is permissible to choose one's employment, to abandon the
wire nail, the
roly-poly, when it shows signs of being no longer a
pleas-

ure, to score the adjacent magazine with a double line of strokes.
He can
talk, but insolently says nothing. What of it? When one is
frank, one's very
presence is a compliment. It is clear that he can see
the virtue of naturalness, that he is one of those who do not
regard
the published fact as a surrender. As for the disposition

invariably to affront, an animal with claws wants to have to use
them; that eel-like extension of trunk into tail is not an acci-
dent. To
leap, to lengthen out, divide the air—to purloin, to pursue.
To tell the hen: fly over the fence, go in the wrong way in
your perturba-
tion—this is life; to do less would be nothing but dis-
honesty.

Picking and Choosing

Literature is a phase of life. If
    one is afraid of it, the situation is irremediable; if
one approaches it familiarly
    what one says of it is worthless. Words are constructive
when they are true; the opaque allusion — the simulated flight

upward — accomplishes nothing. Why cloud the fact
    that Shaw is self-conscious in the field of sentiment but is
        otherwise re-
warding; that James is all that has been
    said of him, if feeling is profound? It is not Hardy
the distinguished novelist and Hardy the poet, but one man

'interpreting life through the medium of the
    emotions'. If he must give an opinion, it is permissible that the
critic should know what he likes. Gordon
    Craig with his 'this is I' and 'this is mine', with his three
wise men, his 'sad French greens' and his Chinese cherry —
        Gordon Craig, so

inclinational and unashamed — has carried
    the precept of being a good critic, to the last extreme; and
        Burke is a
psychologist — of acute, racoon-
    like curiosity. *Summa diligentia*;
to the humbug, whose name is so amusing — very young and ve-

ry rushed, Caesar crossed the Alps 'on the top of a
    diligence'. We are not daft about the meaning, but this famili-
        arity

with wrong meanings puzzles one. Humming-
   bug, the candles are not wired for electricity.
Small dog, going over the lawn, nipping the linen and saying

that you have a badger—remember Xenophon;
   only the most rudimentary sort of behaviour is necessary
to put us on the scent; 'a right good
   salvo of barks', a few 'strong wrinkles' puckering the
skin between the ears, are all we ask.

England

with its baby rivers and little towns, each with its abbey or its
    cathedral,
with voices—one voice perhaps, echoing through the transept
    —the
criterion of suitability and convenience: and Italy with its equal
shores—contriving an epicureanism from which the grossness
    has been

extracted: and Greece with its goat and its gourds, the nest of
    modified illusions:
and France, the 'chrysalis of the nocturnal butterfly', in
whose products mystery of construction diverts one from what
    was originally one's
object—substance at the core: and the East with its snails, its
    emotional

shorthand and jade cockroaches, its rock crystal and its imper-
    turbability,
all of museum quality: and America where there
is the little old ramshackle victoria in the south, where cigars
    are smoked on the
street in the north; where there are no proof-readers, no silk-
    worms, no digressions;

the wild man's land; grassless, linksless, languageless country in
    which letters are written
not in Spanish, not in Greek, not in Latin, not in shorthand,
but in plain American which cats and dogs can read! The letter
    a in psalm and calm when
pronounced with the sound of *a* in candle, is very noticeable, but

why should continents of misapprehension have to be accounted
for by the
fact? Does it follow that because there are poisonous toadstools
which resemble mushrooms, both are dangerous? In the case of
mettlesomeness which may be
mistaken for appetite, of heat which may appear to be haste, no
con-

clusions may be drawn. To have misapprehended the matter is
to have confessed
that one has not looked far enough. The sublimated wisdom
of China, Egyptian discernment, the cataclysmic torrent of
emotion compressed
in the verbs of the Hebrew language, the books of the man who
is able

to say, 'I envy nobody but him, and him only, who catches
more fish than
I do,'—the flower and fruit of all that noted superi-
ority—should one not have stumbled upon it in America, must
one imagine
that it is not there? It has never been confined to one locality.

When I Buy Pictures

or what is closer to the truth,
when I look at that of which I may regard myself as the imagi-
nary possessor,
I fix upon what would give me pleasure in my average
moments:
the satire upon curiosity in which no more is discernible
than the intensity of the mood;
or quite the opposite—the old thing, the mediaeval decorated
hat-box,
in which there are hounds with waists diminishing like the
waist of the hour-glass,
and deer and birds and seated people;
it may be no more than a square of parquetry; the literal bio-
graphy perhaps,
in letters standing well apart upon a parchment-like expanse;
an artichoke in six varieties of blue; the snipe-legged hierogly-
phic in three parts;
the silver fence protecting Adam's grave, or Michael taking
Adam by the wrist.
Too stern an intellectual emphasis upon this quality or that
detracts from one's enjoyment.
It must not wish to disarm anything; nor may the approved
triumph easily be honoured—
that which is great because something else is small.
It comes to this: of whatever sort it is,
it must be 'lit with piercing glances into the life of things';
it must acknowledge the spiritual forces which have made it.

A Grave

Man looking into the sea,
taking the view from those who have as much right to it as you
    have to it yourself,
it is human nature to stand in the middle of a thing,
but you cannot stand in the middle of this;
the sea has nothing to give but a well excavated grave.
The firs stand in a procession, each with an emerald turkey-foot
    at the top,
reserved as their contours, saying nothing;
repression, however, is not the most obvious characteristic of
    the sea;
the sea is a collector, quick to return a rapacious look.
There are others besides you who have worn that look—
whose expression is no longer a protest; the fish no longer in-
    vestigate them
for their bones have not lasted:
men lower nets, unconscious of the fact that they are desecrat-
    ing a grave,
and row quickly away—the blades of the oars
moving together like the feet of water-spiders as if there were
    no such thing as death.
The wrinkles progress upon themselves in a phalanx—beautiful
    under networks of foam,
and fade breathlessly while the sea rustles in and out of the sea-
    weed;
the birds swim through the air at top speed, emitting cat-calls
    as heretofore—
the tortoise-shell scourges about the feet of the cliffs, in motion
    beneath them;

and the ocean, under the pulsation of lighthouse and noise of
     bell-buoys,
advances as usual, looking as if it were not that ocean in which
     dropped things are bound to sink—
in which if they turn and twist, it is neither with volition nor
     consciousness.

Those Various Scalpels,

those
various sounds consistently indistinct, like intermingled echoes
    struck from thin glasses successively at random—the
        inflection disguised: your hair, the tails of two
    fighting-cocks head to head in stone—like sculptured scimi-
        tars re-
        peating the curve of your ears in reverse order: your eyes,
        flowers of ice

and
snow sown by tearing winds on the cordage of disabled ships;
        your raised hand,
    an ambiguous signature: your cheeks, those rosettes
    of blood on the stone floors of French châteaux, with
    regard to which the guides are so affirmative—those regrets
        of the retoucher on the contemporary stone: your other
        hand,

a
bundle of lances all alike, partly hid by emeralds from Persia
    and the fractional magnificence of Florentine
        goldwork—a collection of little objects—
    sapphires set with emeralds and pearls with a moonstone,
        made fine
        with enamel in gray, yellow, and dragon-fly blue; a
        lemon, a

pear
and three bunches of grapes, tied with silver: your dress, a mag-
        nificent square

cathedral tower of uniform
    and at the same time, diverse appearance—a
species of vertical vineyard rustling in the storm
    of conventional opinion. Are they weapons or scalpels?
      Whetted

to
brilliance by the hard majesty of that sophistication which is su-
    perior to opportunity, these things are rich
      instruments with which to experiment; naturally. But
    why dissect destiny with instruments which
      are more highly specialized than the tissues of destiny itself?

The Labours of Hercules,

To popularize the mule, its neat exterior
expressing the principle of accommodation reduced to a mini-
    mum:
to persuade one of austere taste, proud in the possession of
    home and a musician—
that the piano is a free field for etching; that his 'charming tad-
    pole notes'
belong to the past when one had time to play them:
to persuade those self-wrought Midases of brains
whose fourteen carat ignorance aspires to rise in value
till the sky is the limit,
that excessive conduct augurs disappointment,
that one must not borrow a long white beard and tie it on
and threaten with the scythe of time the casually curious:
to teach the bard with too elastic a selectiveness
that one detects creative power by its capacity to conquer one's
    detachment;
that while it may have more elasticity than logic,
it knows where it is going;
it flies along in a straight line like electricity,
depopulating areas that boast of their remoteness,
to prove to the high priests of caste
that snobbishness is a stupidity,
the best side out, of age-old toadyism,
kissing the feet of the man above,
kicking the face of the man below;
to teach the patron-saints-to-atheists, the Coliseum
meet-me-alone-by-moonlight maudlin troubadour
that kickups for catstrings are not life
nor yet appropriate to death—that we are sick of the earth,

sick of the pig-sty, wild geese and wild men;
to convince snake-charming controversialists
that it is one thing to change one's mind,
another to eradicate it—that one keeps on knowing
'that the Negro is not brutal,
that the Jew is not greedy,
that the Oriental is not immoral,
that the German is not a Hun'.

New York

the savage's romance,
accreted where we need the space for commerce—
the centre of the wholesale fur trade,
starred with tepees of ermine and peopled with foxes,
the long guard-hairs waving two inches beyond the body of
    the pelt;
the ground dotted with deer-skins—white with white spots,
'as satin needlework in a single colour may carry a varied
    pattern',
and wilting eagle's-down compacted by the wind;
and picardels of beaver-skin; white ones alert with snow.
It is a far cry from the 'queen full of jewels'
and the beau with the muff,
from the gilt coach shaped like a perfume-bottle,
to the conjunction of the Monongahela and the Allegheny,
and the scholastic philosophy of the wilderness
to combat which one must stand outside and laugh
since to go in is to be lost.
It is not the dime-novel exterior,
Niagara Falls, the calico horses and the war canoe;
it is not that 'if the fur is not finer than such as one sees others
    wear,
one would rather be without it'—
that estimated in raw meat and berries, we could feed the uni-
    verse;
it is not the atmosphere of ingenuity,
the otter, the beaver, the puma skins
without shooting-irons or dogs;
it is not the plunder,
but 'accessibility to experience'.

People's Surroundings

They answer one's questions,
a deal table compact with the wall;
in this dried bone of arrangement
one's 'natural promptness' is compressed, not crowded out;
one's style is not lost in such simplicity.

The palace furniture, so old fashioned, so old fashionable;
Sèvres china and the fireplace dogs—
bronze dromios with pointed ears, as obsolete as pugs;
one has one's preference in the matter of bad furniture,
and this is not one's choice.

The vast indestructible necropolis
of composite Yawman-Erbe separable units;
the steel, the oak, the glass, the Poor Richard publications
containing the public secrets of efficiency
on paper so thin that 'one thousand four hundred and twenty
        pages make one inch',
exclaiming, so to speak, When you take my time, you take
        something I had meant to use;

the highway hid by fir-trees in rhododendron twenty feet
        deep,
the peacocks, hand-forged gates, old Persian velvet,
roses outlined in pale black on an ivory ground,
the pierced iron shadows of the cedars,
Chinese carved glass, old Waterford,
lettered ladies; landscape gardening twisted into permanence;

straight lines over such great distances as one finds in Utah or in
        Texas,

where people do not have to be told
that a good brake is as important as a good motor;
where by means of extra sense-cells in the skin
they can, like trout, smell what is coming—
those cool sirs with the explicit sensory apparatus of common
  sense,
who know the exact distance between two points as the crow
  flies;
there is something attractive about a mind that moves in a
  straight line—
the municipal bat-roost of mosquito warfare, concrete statuary,
medicaments for instant beauty in the hands of all,
and that live wire, the American string quartette;
these are questions more than answers,

and Bluebeard's Tower above the coral-reefs,
the magic mouse-trap closing on all points of the compass,
capping like petrified surf the furious azure of the bay,
where there is no dust, and life is like a lemon-leaf,
a green piece of tough translucent parchment,
where the crimson, the copper, and the Chinese vermilion of
  the poincianas
set fire to the masonry and turquoise blues refute the clock;
this dungeon with odd notions of hospitality,
with its 'chessmen carved out of moonstones',
its mocking-birds, fringed lilies, and hibiscus,
its black butterflies with blue half circles on their wings,
tan goats with onyx ears, its lizards glittering and without
  thickness,

like splashes of fire and silver on the pierced turquoise of the
  lattices
and the acacia-like lady shivering at the touch of a hand,
lost in a small collision of the orchids—
dyed quicksilver let fall

to disappear like an obedient chameleon in fifty shades of
    mauve and amethyst.
Here where the mind of this establishment has come to the con-
    clusion
that it would be impossible to revolve about oneself too much,
sophistication has, 'like an escalator', 'cut the nerve of pro-
    gress'.
In these non-committal, personal-impersonal expressions of
    appearance,
the eye knows what to skip;
the physiognomy of conduct must not reveal the skeleton;
'a setting must not have the air of being one',
yet with x-ray-like inquisitive intensity upon it, the surfaces go
    back;
the interfering fringes of expression are but a stain on what
    stands out,
there is neither up nor down to it;
we see the exterior and the fundamental structure—
captains of armies, cooks, carpenters,
cutlers, gamesters, surgeons and armourers,
lapidaries, silkmen, glovers, fiddlers and ballad-singers,
sextons of churches, dyers of black cloth, hostlers and chimney-
    sweeps,
queens, countesses, ladies, emperors, travellers and mariners,
dukes, princes and gentlemen,
in their respective places—
camps, forges and battlefields,
conventions, oratories and wardrobes,
dens, deserts, railway stations, asylums and places where engines
    are made,
shops, prisons, brickyards and altars of churches—
in magnificent places clean and decent,
castles, palaces, dining-halls, theatres and imperial audience-
    chambers.

Snakes, Mongooses, Snake-Charmers, and the Like

I have a friend who would give a price for those long fingers all
    of one length—
those hideous bird's claws, for that exotic asp and the mon-
    goose—
products of the country in which everything is hard work, the
    country of the grass-getter,
the torch-bearer, the dog-servant, the messenger-bearer, the
    holy-man.
Engrossed in this distinguished worm nearly as wild and as
    fierce as the day it was caught,
he gazes as if incapable of looking at anything with a view to
    analysis.
'The slight snake rippling quickly through the grass,
the leisurely tortoise with its pied back,
the chameleon passing from twig to stone, from stone to
    straw',
lit his imagination at one time; his admiration now converges
    upon this.
Thick, not heavy, it stands up from its travelling-basket,
the essentially Greek, the plastic, animal all of a piece from nose
    to tail;
one is compelled to look at it as at the shadows of the alps
imprisoning in their folds like flies in amber, the rhythms of the
    skating rink.
This animal to which from the earliest times, importance has
    attached,
fine as its worshippers have said—for what was it invented?
To show that when intelligence in its pure form
has embarked on a train of thought which is unproductive, it
    will come back?

We do not know; the only positive thing about it is its shape; but why protest?

The passion for setting people right is in itself an afflictive disease.

Distaste which takes no credit to itself is best.

Bowls

on the green
with lignum vitae balls and ivory markers,
the pins planted in wild duck formation,
and quickly dispersed—
by this survival of ancient punctilio
in the manner of Chinese lacquer carving,
layer after layer exposed by certainty of touch and unhurried
    incision
so that only so much colour shall be revealed as is necessary to
    the picture,
I learn that we are precisians,
not citizens of Pompeii arrested in action
as a cross-section of one's correspondence would seem to imply.
Renouncing a policy of boorish indifference
to everything that has been said since the days of Matilda,
I shall purchase an etymological dictionary of modern English
that I may understand what is written,
and like the ant and the spider
returning from time to time to headquarters,
shall answer the question
'why do I like winter better than I like summer?'
and acknowledge that it does not make me sick
to look playwrights and poets and novelists straight in the face—
that I feel just the same;
and I shall write to the publisher of the magazine
which will 'appear the first day of the month
and disappear before one has had time to buy it
unless one takes proper precaution',
and make an effort to please—
since he who gives quickly gives twice
in nothing so much as in a letter.

Marriage

This institution,
perhaps one should say enterprise
out of respect for which
one says one need not change one's mind
about a thing one has believed in,
requiring public promises
of one's intention
to fulfil a private obligation:
I wonder what Adam and Eve
think of it by this time,
this firegilt steel
alive with goldenness;
how bright it shows—
'of circular traditions and impostures,
committing many spoils',
requiring all one's criminal ingenuity
to avoid!
Psychology which explains everything
explains nothing,
and we are still in doubt.
Eve: beautiful woman—
I have seen her
when she was so handsome
she gave me a start,
able to write simultaneously
in three languages—
English, German and French—
and talk in the meantime;
equally positive in demanding a commotion
and in stipulating quiet:

'I should like to be alone;'
to which the visitor replies,
'I should like to be alone;
why not be alone together?'
Below the incandescent stars
below the incandescent fruit,
the strange experience of beauty;
its existence is too much;
it tears one to pieces
and each fresh wave of consciousness
is poison.
'See her, see her in this common world',
the central flaw
in that first crystal-fine experiment,
this amalgamation which can never be more
than an interesting impossibility,
describing it
as 'that strange paradise
unlike flesh, stones,
gold or stately buildings,
the choicest piece of my life:
the heart rising
in its estate of peace
as a boat rises
with the rising of the water';
constrained in speaking of the serpent—
shed snakeskin in the history of politeness
not to be returned to again—
that invaluable accident
exonerating Adam.
And he has beauty also;
it's distressing—the O thou
to whom from whom,
without whom nothing—Adam;

'something feline,
something colubrine'—how true!
a crouching mythological monster
in that Persian miniature of emerald mines,
raw silk—ivory white, snow white,
oyster white and six others—
that paddock full of leopards and giraffes—
long lemon-yellow bodies
sown with trapezoids of blue.
Alive with words,
vibrating like a cymbal
touched before it has been struck,
he has prophesied correctly—
the industrious waterfall,
'the speedy stream
which violently bears all before it,
at one time silent as the air
and now as powerful as the wind'.
'Treading chasms
on the uncertain footing of a spear',
forgetting that there is in woman
a quality of mind
which as an instinctive manifestation
is unsafe,
he goes on speaking
in a formal customary strain,
of 'past states, the present state,
seals, promises,
the evil one suffered,
the good one enjoys,
hell, heaven,
everything convenient
to promote one's joy'.
In him a state of mind

perceives what it was not
intended that he should;
'he experiences a solemn joy
in seeing that he has become an idol'.
Plagued by the nightingale
in the new leaves,
with its silence—
not its silence but its silences,
he says of it:
'It clothes me with a shirt of fire.'
'He dares not clap his hands
to make it go on
lest it should fly off;
if he does nothing, it will sleep;
if he cries out, it will not understand.'
Unnerved by the nightingale
and dazzled by the apple,
impelled by 'the illusion of a fire
effectual to extinguish fire',
compared with which
the shining of the earth
is but deformity—a fire
'as high as deep
as bright as broad
as long as life itself',
he stumbles over marriage,
'a very trivial object indeed'
to have destroyed the attitude
in which he stood—
the ease of the philosopher
unfathered by a woman.
Unhelpful Hymen!
a kind of overgrown cupid
reduced to insignificance

by the mechanical advertising
parading as involuntary comment,
by that experiment of Adam's
with ways out but no way in—
the ritual of marriage,
augmenting all its lavishness;
its fiddle-head ferns,
lotus flowers, opuntias, white dromedaries,
its hippopotamus—
nose and mouth combined
in one magnificent hopper—
its snake and the potent apple.
He tells us
that 'for love that will
gaze an eagle blind,
that is with Hercules
climbing the trees
in the garden of the Hesperides,
from forty-five to seventy
is the best age',
commending it
as a fine art, as an experiment,
a duty or as merely recreation.
One must not call him ruffian
nor friction a calamity—
the fight to be affectionate:
'no truth can be fully known
until it has been tried
by the tooth of disputation'.
The blue panther with black eyes,
the basalt panther with blue eyes,
entirely graceful—
one must give them the path—
the black obsidian Diana

who 'darkeneth her countenance
as a bear doth',
the spiked hand
that has an affection for one
and proves it to the bone,
impatient to assure you
that impatience is the mark of independence,
not of bondage.
'Married people often look that way'—
'seldom and cold, up and down,
mixed and malarial
with a good day and bad'.
'When do we feed?'
We occidentals are so unemotional,
we quarrel as we feed;
self lost, the irony preserved
in 'the Ahasuerus *tête-à-tête* banquet'
with its small orchids like snakes' tongues,
with its 'good monster, lead the way',
with little laughter
and munificence of humour
in that quixotic atmosphere of frankness
in which, 'four o'clock does not exist,
but at five o'clock
the ladies in their imperious humility
are ready to receive you';
in which experience attests
that men have power
and sometimes one is made to feel it.
He says, 'What monarch would not blush
to have a wife
with hair like a shaving-brush?
The fact of woman
is "not the sound of the flute

but very poison".'
She says, 'Men are monopolists
of "stars, garters, buttons
and other shining baubles"—
unfit to be the guardians
of another person's happiness.'
He says, 'These mummies
must be handled carefully—
"the crumbs from a lion's meal,
a couple of shins and the bit of an ear";
turn to the letter M
and you will find
that "a wife is a coffin",
that severe object
with the pleasing geometry
stipulating space not people,
refusing to be buried
and uniquely disappointing,
revengefully wrought in the attitude
of an adoring child
to a distinguished parent.'
She says, 'This butterfly,
this waterfly, this nomad
that has "proposed
to settle on my hand for life".—
What can one do with it?
There must have been more time
in Shakespeare's day
to sit and watch a play.
You know so many artists who are fools.'
He says, 'You know so many fools
who are not artists.'
The fact forgot
that 'some have merely rights

while some have obligations',
he loves himself so much,
he can permit himself
no rival in that love.
She loves herself so much,
she cannot see herself enough—
a statuette of ivory on ivory,
the logical last touch
to an expansive splendour
earned as wages for work done:
one is not rich but poor
when one can always seem so right.
What can one do for them—
these savages
condemned to disaffect
all those who are not visionaries
alert to undertake the silly task
of making people noble?
This model of petrine fidelity
who 'leaves her peaceful husband
only because she has seen enough of him'—
that orator reminding you,
'I am yours to command.'
'Everything to do with love is mystery;
it is more than a day's work
to investigate this science.'
One sees that it is rare—
that striking grasp of opposites
opposed each to the other, not to unity,
which in cycloid inclusiveness
has dwarfed the demonstration
of Columbus with the egg—
a triumph of simplicity—
that charitive Euroclydon

of frightening disinterestedness
which the world hates,
admitting:

>'I am such a cow,
>if I had a sorrow,
>I should feel it a long time;
>I am not one of those
>who have a great sorrow
>in the morning
>and a great joy at noon;'

which says: 'I have encountered it
among those unpretentious
protégés of wisdom,
where seeming to parade
as the debater and the Roman,
the statesmanship
of an archaic Daniel Webster
persists to their simplicity of temper
as the essence of the matter:

>"Liberty and union
>now and forever;"

the Book on the writing-table;
the hand in the breast-pocket.'

Novices

anatomize their work
in the sense in which Will Honeycomb was jilted by a duchess;
the little assumptions of the scared ego confusing the issue
so that they do not know 'whether it is the buyer or the seller
 who gives the money'—
an abstruse idea plain to none but the artist,
the only seller who buys, and holds on to the money.
Because one expresses oneself and entitles it wisdom, one is not
 a fool. What an idea!
'Dracontine cockatrices, perfect and poisonous from the be-
 ginning',
they present themselves as a contrast to sea-serpented regions
 'unlit by the half-lights of more conscious art'.

Acquiring at thirty what at sixty they will be trying to
 forget,
blind to the right word, deaf to satire
which like 'the smell of the cypress strengthens the nerves of
 the brain',
averse from the antique
with 'that tinge of sadness about it which a reflective mind
 always feels,
it is so little and so much'—
they write the sort of thing that would in their judgment interest
 a lady;
curious to know if we do not adore each letter of the alphabet
 that goes to make a word of it—
according to the Act of Congress, the sworn statement of the
 treasurer and all the rest of it—
the counterpart to what we are:

stupid man; men are strong and no one pays any attention:
stupid woman; women have charm, and how annoying they
    can be.
Yes, 'the authors are wonderful people, particularly those that
    write the most',
the masters of all languages, the supertadpoles of expression.
Accustomed to the recurring phosphorescence of antiquity,
the 'much noble vagueness and indefinite jargon' of Plato,
the lucid movements of the royal yacht upon the learned scen-
    ery of Egypt—
king, steward, and harper, seated amidships while the jade and
    the rock crystal course about in solution,

their suavity surmounts the surf—
the willowy wit, the transparent equation of Isaiah, Jeremiah,
    Ezekiel, Daniel.
Bored by 'the detailless perspective of the sea', reiterative and
    naïve,
and its chaos of rocks—the stuffy remarks of the Hebrews—
the good and alive young men demonstrate the assertion
that it is not necessary to be associated with that which has
    bored one;
they have never made a statement which they found so easy to
    prove—
'split like a glass against a wall'
in this 'precipitate of dazzling impressions,
the spontaneous unforced passion of the Hebrew language—
an abyss of verbs full of reverberations and tempestuous
    energy'
in which action perpetuates action and angle is at variance with
    angle
till submerged by the general action;
obscured by 'fathomless suggestions of colour',
by incessantly panting lines of green, white with concussion,

in this drama of water against rocks—this 'ocean of hurrying
    consonants'
with its 'great livid stains like long slabs of green marble',
its 'flashing lances of perpendicular lightning' and 'molten fires
    swallowed up',
'with foam on its barriers',
'crashing itself out in one long hiss of spray'.

An Octopus

of ice. Deceptively reserved and flat,
it lies 'in grandeur and in mass'
beneath a sea of shifting snow-dunes;
dots of cyclamen-red and maroon on its clearly defined pseudo-
    podia
made of glass that will bend—a much needed invention—
comprising twenty-eight ice-fields from fifty to five hundred
    feet thick,
of unimagined delicacy.
'Picking periwinkles from the cracks'
or killing prey with the concentric crushing rigour of the
    python,
it hovers forward 'spider fashion
on its arms' misleadingly like lace;
its 'ghostly pallor changing
to the green metallic tinge of an anemone-starred pool'.
The fir-trees, in 'the magnitude of their root systems',
rise aloof from these manoeuvres 'creepy to behold',
austere specimens of our American royal families,
'each like the shadow of the one beside it.
The rock seems frail compared with their dark energy of life',
its vermilion and onyx and manganese-blue interior expensive-
    ness
left at the mercy of the weather;
'stained transversely by iron where the water drips down',
recognized by its plants and its animals.
Completing a circle,
you have been deceived into thinking that you have progressed,
under the polite needles of the larches
'hung to filter, not to intercept the sunlight'—

met by tightly wattled spruce-twigs
'conformed to an edge like clipped cypress
as if no branch could penetrate the cold beyond its company';
and dumps of gold and silver ore enclosing The Goat's Mirror—
that lady-fingerlike depression in the shape of the left human
    foot,
which prejudices you in favour of itself
before you have had time to see the others;
its indigo, pea-green, blue-green, and turquoise,
from a hundred to two hundred feet deep,
'merging in irregular patches in the middle lake
where, like gusts of a storm
obliterating the shadows of the fir-trees, the wind makes lanes
    of ripples'.
What spot could have merits of equal importance
for bears, elk, deer, wolves, goats, and ducks?
Pre-empted by their ancestors,
this is the property of the exacting porcupine,
and of the rat 'slipping along to its burrow in the swamp
or pausing on high ground to smell the heather';
of 'thoughtful beavers
making drains which seem the work of careful men with
    shovels',
and of the bears inspecting unexpectedly
ant-hills and berry-bushes.
Composed of calcium gems and alabaster pillars,
topaz, tourmaline crystals and amethyst quartz,
their den is somewhere else, concealed in the confusion
of 'blue forests thrown together with marble and jasper and
    agate
as if whole quarries had been dynamited'.
And farther up, in stag-at-bay position
as a scintillating fragment of these terrible stalagmites,
stands the goat,

its eye fixed on the waterfall which never seems to fall—
an endless skein swayed by the wind,
immune to force of gravity in the perspective of the peaks.
A special antelope
acclimated to 'grottoes from which issue penetrating draughts
which make you wonder why you came',
it stands its ground
on cliffs the colour of the clouds, of petrified white vapour—
black feet, eyes, nose, and horns, engraved on dazzling ice-
    fields,
the ermine body on the crystal peak;
the sun kindling its shoulders to maximum heat like acetylene,
    dyeing them white—
upon this antique pedestal,
'a mountain with those graceful lines which prove it a volcano',
its top a complete cone like Fujiyama's
till an explosion blew it off.
Distinguished by a beauty
of which 'the visitor dare never fully speak at home
for fear of being stoned as an impostor',
Big Snow Mountain is the home of a diversity of creatures:
those who 'have lived in hotels
but who now live in camps—who prefer to';
the mountain guide evolving from the trapper,
'in two pairs of trousers, the outer one older,
wearing slowly away from the feet to the knees';
'the nine-striped chipmunk
running with unmammal-like agility along a log';
the water ouzel
with 'its passion for rapids and high-pressured falls',
building under the arch of some tiny Niagara;
the white-tailed ptarmigan 'in winter solid white,
feeding on heather-bells and alpine buckwheat';
and the eleven eagles of the west,

'fond of the spring fragrance and the winter colours',
used to the unegoistic action of the glaciers
and 'several hours of frost every midsummer night'.
'They make a nice appearance, don't they',
happy seeing nothing?
Perched on treacherous lava and pumice—
those unadjusted chimney-pots and cleavers
which stipulate 'names and addresses of persons to notify
in case of disaster'—
they hear the roar of ice and supervise the water
winding slowly through the cliffs,
the road 'climbing like the thread
which forms the groove around a snail-shell,
doubling back and forth until where snow begins, it ends'.
No 'deliberate wide-eyed wistfulness' is here
among the boulders sunk in ripples and white water
where 'when you hear the best wild music of the forest
it is sure to be a marmot',
the victim on some slight observatory,
of 'a struggle between curiosity and caution',
inquiring what has scared it:
a stone from the moraine descending in leaps,
another marmot, or the spotted ponies with glass eyes,
brought up on frosty grass and flowers
and rapid draughts of ice-water.
Instructed none knows how, to climb the mountain,
by business men who as totemic scenery of Canada,
require for recreation
three hundred and sixty-five holidays in the year,
these conspicuously spotted little horses are peculiar;
hard to discern among the birch-trees, ferns, and lily-pads,
avalanche lilies, Indian paint-brushes,
bear's ears and kittentails,
and miniature cavalcades of chlorophylless fungi

magnified in profile on the mossbeds like moonstones in the
    water;
the cavalcade of calico competing
with the original American menagerie of styles
among the white flowers of the rhododendron surmounting
    rigid leaves
upon which moisture works its alchemy,
transmuting verdure into onyx.
Larkspur, blue pincushions, blue peas, and lupin;
white flowers with white, and red with red;
the blue ones 'growing close together
so that patches of them look like blue water in the distance';
this arrangement of colours
as in Persian designs of hard stones with enamel,
forms a pleasing equation—
a diamond outside, and inside, a white dot;
on the outside, a ruby; inside, a red dot;
black spots balanced with black
in the woodlands where fires have run over the ground—
separated by aspens, cat's paws, and woolly sunflowers,
fireweed, asters, and Goliath thistles
'flowering at all altitudes as multiplicitous as barley',
like pink sapphires in the pavement of the glistening plateau.
Inimical to 'bristling, puny, swearing men
equipped with saws and axes',
this treacherous glass mountain
admires gentians, lady-slippers, harebells, mountain dryads,
and 'Calypso, the goat flower—
that greenish orchid fond of snow'—
anomalously nourished upon shelving glacial ledges
where climbers have not gone or have gone timidly,
'the one resting his nerves while the other advanced',
on this volcano with the blue jay, her principal companion.
'Hopping stiffly on sharp feet' like miniature ice-hacks—

'secretive, with a look of wisdom and distinction, but a villain,
fond of human society or the crumbs that go with it',
he knows no Greek,
'that pride-producing language',
in which 'rashness is rendered innocuous, and error exposed
by the collision of knowledge with knowledge'.

'Like happy souls in Hell', enjoying mental difficulties,
the grasshoppers of Greece
amused themselves with delicate behaviour
because it was 'so noble and so fair';
not practised in adapting their intelligence
to eagle-traps and snow-shoes,
to alpenstocks and other toys contrived by those
'alive to the advantage of invigorating pleasures'.
Bows, arrows, oars, and paddles, for which trees provide the
        wood,
in new countries are more eloquent than elsewhere—
augmenting the assertion that, essentially humane,
'the forest affords wood for dwellings and by its beauty stimu-
        lates
the moral vigour of its citizens'.
The Greeks liked smoothness, distrusting what was back
of what could not be clearly seen,
resolving with benevolent conclusiveness,
'complexities which still will be complexities
as long as the world lasts';
ascribing what we clumsily call happiness,
to 'an accident or a quality,
a spiritual substance or the soul itself,
an act, a disposition, or a habit,
or a habit infused, to which the soul has been persuaded,
or something distinct from a habit, a power—'
such power as Adam had and we are still devoid of.

'Emotionally sensitive, their hearts were hard';
their wisdom was remote
from that of these odd oracles of cool official sarcasm,
upon this game preserve
where 'guns, nets, seines, traps and explosives,
hired vehicles, gambling and intoxicants are prohibited;
disobedient persons being summarily removed
and not allowed to return without permission in writing'.
It is self-evident
that it is frightful to have everything afraid of one;
that one must do as one is told
and eat 'rice, prunes, dates, raisins, hardtack, and tomatoes'
if one would 'conquer the main peak' of Mount Tacoma,
this fossil flower concise without a shiver,
intact when it is cut,
damned for its sacrosanct remoteness—
like Henry James 'damned by the public for decorum';
not decorum, but restraint;
it was the love of doing hard things
that rebuffed and wore them out—a public out of sympathy
        with neatness.
Neatness of finish! Neatness of finish!
Relentless accuracy is the nature of this octopus
with its capacity for fact.
'Creeping slowly as with meditated stealth,
its arms seeming to approach from all directions',
it receives one under winds that 'tear the snow to bits
and hurl it like a sandblast
shearing off twigs and loose bark from the trees'.
Is 'tree' the word for these things
'flat on the ground like vines'?
some 'bent in a half circle with branches on one side
suggesting dust-brushes, not trees;
some finding strength in union, forming little stunted groves,

their flattened mats of branches shrunk in trying to escape'
from the hard mountain 'planed by ice and polished by the
   wind'—
the white volcano with no weather side;
the lightning flashing at its base,
rain falling in the valleys, and snow falling on the peak—
the glassy octopus symmetrically pointed,
its claw cut by the avalanche
'with a sound like the crack of a rifle,
in a curtain of powdered snow launched like a waterfall'.

Sea Unicorns and Land Unicorns

with their respective lions—
'mighty monoceroses with immeasured tayles'—
these are those very animals
described by the cartographers of 1539,
defiantly revolving
in such a way that
the long keel of white exhibited in tumbling,
disperses giant weeds
and those sea snakes whose forms looped in the foam, 'disquiet
    shippers'.
Not ignorant of how a voyager obtained the horn of a sea uni-
    corn
to give Queen Elizabeth,
who thought it worth a hundred thousand pounds,
they persevere in swimming where they like,
finding the place where lions live in herds,
strewn on the beach like stones with lesser stones—
and bears are white;
discovering Antarctica, its penguin kings and icy spires,
and Sir John Hawkins' Florida
'abounding in land unicorns and lions;
since where the one is,
its arch enemy cannot be missing'.
Thus personalities by nature much opposed,
can be combined in such a way
that when they do agree, their unanimity is great,
'in politics, in trade, law, sport, religion,
china-collecting, tennis, and church going'.
You have remarked this fourfold combination of strange
    animals,

upon embroideries
enwrought with 'polished garlands' of agreeing indifference—
thorns, 'myrtle rods, and shafts of bay',
'cobwebs, and knotts, and mulberries'
of lapis-lazuli and pomegranate and malachite—
Britannia's sea unicorn with its rebellious child
now ostentatiously indigenous of the new English coast;
and its land lion oddly tolerant of those pacific counterparts to it,
the water lions of the west.
This is a strange fraternity—these sea lions and land lions,
land unicorns and sea unicorns:
the lion civilly rampant,
tame and concessive like the long-tailed bear of Ecuador—
the lion standing up against this screen of woven air
which is the forest:
the unicorn also, on its hind legs in reciprocity.
A puzzle to the hunters, is this haughtiest of beasts,
to be distinguished from those born without a horn,
in use like Saint Jerome's tame lion, as domestics;
rebelling proudly at the dogs
which are dismayed by the chain lightning
playing at them from its horn—
the dogs persistent in pursuit of it as if it could be caught,
'deriving agreeable terror' from its 'moonbeam throat'
on fire like its white coat and unconsumed as if of salamander's
    skin.
So wary as to disappear for centuries and reappear,
yet never to be caught,
the unicorn has been preserved
by an unmatched device
wrought like the work of expert blacksmiths,
with which nothing can compare—
this animal of that one horn
throwing itself upon which head foremost from a cliff,

it walks away unharmed;
proficient in this feat which, like Herodotus,
I have not seen except in pictures.
Thus this strange animal with its miraculous elusiveness,
has come to be unique,
'impossible to take alive',
tamed only by a lady inoffensive like itself—
as curiously wild and gentle;
'as straight and slender as the crest,
or antlet of the one-beam'd beast'.
Upon the printed page,
also by word of mouth,
we have a record of it all
and how, unfearful of deceit,
etched like an equine monster on an old celestial map,
beside a cloud or dress of Virgin-Mary blue,
improved 'all over slightly with snakes of Venice gold,
and silver, and some O's',
the unicorn 'with pavon high', approaches eagerly;
until engrossed by what appears of this strange enemy,
upon the map, 'upon her lap',
its 'mild wild head doth lie'.

The Monkey Puzzle

A kind of monkey or pine-lemur
not of interest to the monkey,
in a kind of Flaubert's Carthage, it defies one—
this 'Paduan cat with lizard', this 'tiger in a bamboo thicket'.
'An interwoven somewhat', it will not come out.
Ignore the Foo dog and it is forthwith more than a dog,
its tail superimposed upon itself in a complacent half spiral,
incidentally so witty;
but this pine-tree—this pine-tiger, is a tiger, not a dog.
It knows that if a nomad may have dignity,
Gibraltar has had more—
that 'it is better to be lonely than unhappy'.
A conifer contrived in imitation of the glyptic work of jade and
    hard-stone cutters,
a true curio in this bypath of curio collecting,
it is worth its weight in gold, but no one takes it
from these woods in which society's not knowing is colossal,
the lion's ferocious chrysanthemum head seeming kind in com-
    parison.
This porcupine-quilled, complicated starkness—
this is beauty—'a certain proportion in the skeleton which gives
    the best results'.
One is at a loss, however, to know why it should be here,
in this morose part of the earth—
to account for its origin at all;
but we prove, we do not explain our birth.

Injudicious Gardening

If yellow betokens infidelity,
   I am an infidel.
     I could not bear a yellow rose ill will
     Because books said that yellow boded ill,
   White promised well;

However, your particular possession—
   The sense of privacy
     In what you did—deflects from your estate
     Offending eyes, and will not tolerate
   Effrontery.

Is Your Town Nineveh?

Why so desolate?
  in phantasmagoria about fishes,
    what disgusts you? Could
      not all personal upheaval in
        the name of freedom, be tabooed?

Is it Nineveh
  and are you Jonah
    in the sweltering east wind of your wishes?
      I myself have stood
        there by the Aquarium, looking
          at the Statue of Liberty.

To Military Progress

You use your mind
Like a millstone to grind
    Chaff.
You polish it
And with your warped wit
    Laugh

At your torso,
Prostrate where the crow
    Falls
On such faint hearts
As its god imparts,
    Calls

And claps its wings
Till the tumult brings
    More
Black minute-men
To revive again,
    War

At little cost.
They cry for the lost
    Head
And seek their prize
Till the evening sky's
    Red.

An Egyptian Pulled Glass Bottle in the
Shape of a Fish

Here we have thirst
And patience, from the first,
   And art, as in a wave held up for us to see
   In its essential perpendicularity;

Not brittle but
Intense—the spectrum, that
   Spectacular and nimble animal the fish,
   Whose scales turn aside the sun's sword with their polish.

To a Steam Roller

The illustration
is nothing to you without the application.
    You lack half wit. You crush all the particles down
        into close conformity, and then walk back and forth on
            them.

Sparkling chips of rock
are crushed down to the level of the parent block.
    Were not 'impersonal judgment in aesthetic
        matters, a metaphysical impossibility', you

might fairly achieve
it. As for butterflies, I can hardly conceive
    of one's attending upon you, but to question
        the congruence of the complement is vain, if it exists.

To a Snail

If 'compression is the first grace of style',
you have it. Contractility is a virtue
as modesty is a virtue.
It is not the acquisition of any one thing
that is able to adorn,
or the incidental quality that occurs
as a concomitant of something well said,
that we value in style,
but the principle that is hid:
in the absence of feet, 'a method of conclusions';
'a knowledge of principles',
in the curious phenomenon of your occipital horn.

'The Bricks are Fallen Down, We Will Build with Hewn Stones. The Sycamores are Cut Down, We Will Change to Cedars'

In what sense shall we be able to
    secure to ourselves peace and do as they did—
    who, when they were not able to rid
        themselves of war, cast out fear?
            They did not say: 'We shall not be brought
                into subjection by the naughtiness of the sea;
though we have "defeated ourselves with
    false balances" and laid weapons in the scale,
    glory shall spring from inglory; hail,
        flood, earthquake, and famine shall
            not intimidate us nor shake the
                foundations of our inalienable energy.'

'Nothing Will Cure the Sick Lion but to Eat an Ape'

Perceiving that in the masked ball
attitude, there is a hollowness
that beauty's light momentum can't redeem;
   since disproportionate satisfaction anywhere
   lacks a proportionate air,

he let us know without offence
by his hands' denunciatory
upheaval, that he despised the fashion
   of curing us with an ape—making it his care
   to smother us with fresh air.

To the Peacock of France

In 'taking charge of your possessions when you saw them' you
             became a golden jay.
Scaramouche said you charmed his charm away,
  But not his colour? Yes, his colour when you liked.
  Of chiselled setting and black-opalescent dye,
    You were the jewelry of sense;
      Of sense, not licence; you but trod the pace
      Of liberty in market-place
        And court. Molière,
          The huggermugger repertory of your first adventure,
           is your own affair.
'Anchorites do not dwell in theatres,' and peacocks do not
            flourish in a cell.
Why make distinctions? The results were well
  When you were on the boards; nor were your triumphs
         bought
  At horrifying sacrifice of stringency.
    You hated sham; you ranted up
      And down through the conventions of excess;
      Nor did the King love you the less
        Nor did the world,
         In whose chief interest and for whose spontaneous de-
          light, your broad tail was unfurled.

The Past is the Present

If external action is effete
   and rhyme is outmoded,
     I shall revert to you,
   Habakkuk, as on a recent occasion I was goaded
       into doing by XY, who was speaking of unrhymed verse.
This man said—I think that I repeat
   his identical words:
     'Hebrew poetry is
  prose with a sort of heightened consciousness.' Ecstasy affords
     the occasion and expediency determines the form.

'He Wrote the History Book'

There! You shed a ray
   of whimsicality on a mask of profundity so
      terrific, that I have been dumbfounded by
it oftener than I care to say.
         The book? Titles are chaff.

Authentically
   brief and full of energy, you contribute to your father's
      legibility and are sufficiently
synthetic. Thank you for showing me
      your father's autograph.

Like a Bulrush

or the spike
of a channel-marker or the
moon, he superintended the demolition of his image in
the water by the wind; he did not strike

them at the
time as being different from
any other inhabitant of the water; it was as if he
were a seal in the combined livery
of bird plus
snake; it was as if he knew that
the penguins were not fish, and as if in their bat blindness, they
    did not
realize that he was amphibious.

Sojourn in the Whale

Trying to open locked doors with a sword, threading
   the points of needles, planting shade trees
   upside down; swallowed by the opaqueness of one whom
     the seas
love better than they love you, Ireland—

you have lived and lived on every kind of shortage.
   You have been compelled by hags to spin
   gold thread from straw and have heard men say: 'There is a
     feminine
temperament in direct contrast to

ours which makes her do these things. Circumscribed by a
   heritage of blindness and native
   incompetence, she will become wise and will be forced to
     give
in. Compelled by experience, she

will turn back; water seeks its own level:' and you
   have smiled. 'Water in motion is far
   from level.' You have seen it, when obstacles happened to
     bar
the path, rise automatically.

Silence

My father used to say,
'Superior people never make long visits,
have to be shown Longfellow's grave
nor the glass flowers at Harvard.
Self-reliant like the cat—
that takes its prey to privacy,
the mouse's limp tail hanging like a shoelace from its mouth—
they sometimes enjoy solitude,
and can be robbed of speech
by speech which has delighted them.
The deepest feeling always shows itself in silence;
not in silence, but restraint.'
Nor was he insincere in saying, 'Make my house your inn.'
Inns are not residences.

A Postscript

Dedications imply giving, and we do not care to make a gift of what is insufficient; but in my immediate family there is one 'who thinks in a particular way'; and I should like to add that where there is an effect of thought or pith in these pages, the thinking and often the actual phrases are hers.

M.C.M.

1934

Notes

The Popes' colossal fir-cone of bronze. 'Perforated with holes, it served as a fountain. Its inscription states "P. Cincius P. l. Salvius fecit". See Duff's *Freedmen in the Early Roman Empire.'* *The Periodical,* February, 1929 (Oxford University Press).

Stone locusts. Toilet-box dating from about the twenty-second Egyptian Dynasty. *Illustrated London News,* 26th July, 1930.

The king's cane. Description by J. D. S. Pendlebury. *Illustrated London News,* 19th March, 1932.

Folding bedroom. The portable bed-chamber of Queen Hetepheres presented to her by her son, Cheops. Described by Dr G. A. Reisner. *Illustrated London News,* 7th May, 1932.

'There are little rats called jerboas which run on long hind-legs as thin as a match. The forelimbs are mere tiny hands.' Dr R. L. Ditmars: p. 274, *Strange Animals I Have Known.*

CAMELLIA SABINA

The Abbé Berlèse; Monographie du Genre Camellia (H. Cousin).

Bordeaux merchants have spent a great deal of trouble. *Encyclopaedia Britannica.*

The French are a cruel race, etc. Dr J. Sibley Watson.

A food grape. In Vol. I, *The Epicure's Guide to France* (Thornton Butterworth) Curnonsky and Marcel Rouff quote Monselet: 'Everywhere else you eat grapes which have ripened to make wine. In France you eat grapes which have ripened for the table. They are a product at once of nature and of art.' . . . The bunch 'is covered and uncovered alternately, according to the intensity of the heat, to gild the grapes without scorching them. Those which refuse to ripen – and there are always some – are delicately removed with special scissors, as are also those which have been spoiled by the rain.'

Wild parsnip. Edward W. Nelson, 'Smaller Mammals of North America', *National Geographic Magazine,* May, 1918.

Mouse with a grape. Photograph by Spencer R. Atkinson, *National Geographic Magazine,* February, 1932. 'Carrying a baby in her mouth and a grape in her right forepaw, a round-tailed wood rat took this picture.'

The wire cage. Photograph by Alvin E. Worman of Attleboro, Massachusetts.

NO SWAN SO FINE

'There is no water so still as the dead fountains of Versailles'. Percy Phillip, *New York Times Magazine,* 10th May, 1931.

A pair of Louis XV candelabra with Dresden figures of swans belonging to Lord Balfour.

THE PLUMET BASILISK

Basiliscus Americanus Gray.

Guatavita Lake. Associated with the legend of El Dorado, the Gilded One. The king, painted with gums and powdered with gold-dust as symbolic of the sun, the supreme deity, was each year escorted by his nobles on a raft, to the centre of the lake, in a ceremonial of tribute to the goddess of the lake. Here he washed off his golden coat by plunging into the water while those on the raft and on the shores chanted and threw offerings into the waters – emeralds or objects of gold, silver, or platinum. See A. Hyatt Verrill, *Lost Treasure* (Appleton).

Frank Davis; *The Chinese Dragon. Illustrated London News,* 23rd August, 1930. 'He is the god of Rain, and the Ruler of Rivers, Lakes, and Seas. For six months of the year he hibernates in the depths of the sea, living in beautiful palaces. . . .

'We learn from a book of the T'ang Dynasty that "it may cause itself to become visible or invisible at will, and it can become long or short, and coarse or fine, at its own good pleasure".'

A dragon 'is either born a dragon (and true dragons have nine sons) or becomes one by transformation'. There is a 'legend of the carp that try to climb a certain cataract in the western hills. Those that succeed become dragons.'

The Malay Dragon and the 'basilisks'. W. P. Pycraft, *Illustrated London News,* 6th February, 1932. The basilisk 'will when alarmed drop to the water and scuttle along the surface on its hind-legs. . . . An allied species (Deiropteryx) can not only run along the surface of the water, but can also dive to the bottom, and there find safety till danger is past.'

The Tuatera or Ngarara. In appearance a lizard – with characteristics of the tortoise; on the ribs, uncinate processes like a bird's; and crocodilian features – it is the only living representative of the order Rhynchocephalia. Shown by Captain Stanley Osborne in motion pictures. Cf. *Animals of New Zealand,* by F. W. Hutton and James Drummond (Whitcombe and Tombs).

A fox's bridge. The South American vine suspension bridge.

A seven-hundred-foot chain of gold weighing more than ten tons was being brought from Cuzco, as part of the ransom for Atahualpa. When news of his murder reached those in command of the convoy, they ordered that the chain be hidden, and it has never been found. See A. Hyatt Verrill, *Lost Treasure* (Appleton).

THE FRIGATE PELICAN

Fregata aquila. The Frigate Pelican of Audubon.

Giant tame armadillo. Photograph and description by W. Stephen Thomas of New York.

Red-spotted orchids. The blood, supposedly, of natives slain by Pizarro.

'If I do well, I am blessed,' etc. Hindoo saying.

NINE NECTARINES AND OTHER PORCELAIN

Alphonse de Candolle: *Origin of Cultivated Plants* (Appleton, 1886). 'The Chinese believe the oval peaches which are very red on one side, to be a symbol of long life. . . . According to the work of Chin-noug-king, the peach *Yu* prevents death. If it is not eaten in time, it at least preserves the body from decay until the end of the world.'

'Brown beaks and cheeks.' Anderson Catalogue 2301, to Karl Freund collection sale, 1928.

New York Sun, 2nd July, 1932. *The World To-day,* by Edgar Snow, from Soochow, China; 'An old gentleman of China, whom I met when I first came to this country, volunteered to name for me what he called the "six certainties". He said: "You may be sure that the clearest jade comes from Yarkand, the prettiest flowers from Szechuen, the most fragile porcelain from Kingtehchen, the finest tea from Fukien, the sheerest silk from Hangchow, and the most beautiful women from Soochow". . . .'

The kylin (or Chinese unicorn). Frank Davis: *Illustrated London News,* 7th March, 1931. 'It has the body of a stag, with a single horn, the tail of a cow, horse's hoofs, a yellow belly, and hair of five colours.'

IN THIS AGE OF HARD TRYING

'It is not the business of the gods to bake clay pots.' Dostoievsky.

POETRY

Diary of Tolstoy (Dutton), p. 84. 'Where the boundary between prose and poetry lies, I shall never be able to understand. The question is raised in manuals of style, yet the answer to it lies beyond me. Poetry is verse: prose is not verse. Or else poetry is everything with the exception of business documents and school books.'

'Literalists of the imagination.' Yeats: *Ideas of Good and Evil* (A. H. Bullen), p. 182. 'The limitation of his view was from the very intensity of his vision; he was a too literal realist of imagination, as others are of nature; and because he believed that the figures seen by the mind's eye, when exalted by inspiration, were "eternal existences", symbols of divine essences, he hated every grace of style that might obscure their lineaments.'

PEDANTIC LITERALIST

All excerpts from Richard Baxter: *The Saints' Everlasting Rest* (Lippincott).

IN THE DAYS OF PRISMATIC COLOUR

'Part of it was crawling', etc. Nestor: *Greek Anthology* (Loeb Classical Library), Vol. III, p. 129.

PETER

Cat owned by Miss Magdalen Hueber and Miss Maria Weniger.

PICKING AND CHOOSING

Feeling. T. S. Eliot: 'In Memory', in *The Little Review*, August, 1918. 'James's critical genius comes out most tellingly in his mastery over, his baffling escape from Ideas; a mastery and an escape which are perhaps the last test of a superior intelligence. He had a mind so fine that no idea could violate it. . . . In England ideas run wild and pasture on the emotions; instead of thinking with our feelings (a very different thing), we corrupt our feelings with ideas; we produce the political, the emotional idea, evading sensation and thought.'

'Sad French greens'. *Compleat Angler.*

'Top of a *diligence*'. Preparatory school boy translating Caesar. Recollected by Mr E. H. Kellogg.

'A right good salvo of barks'; 'strong wrinkles'. Xenophon's *Cynegeticus.*

ENGLAND

'Chrysalis of the nocturnal butterfly'. Erté.

'I envy nobody', etc. *Compleat Angler.*

WHEN I BUY PICTURES

'A silver fence was erected by Constantine to enclose the grave of Adam.' *Literary Digest*, 5th January, 1918; descriptive paragraph with photograph.

'Lit by piercing glances', etc. A. R. Gordon: *the Poets of The Old Testament* (Hodder and Stoughton).

THE LABOURS OF HERCULES

'Charming tadpole notes'. *The London Spectator.*

'The negro is not brutal', etc. The Reverend J. W. Darr.

NEW YORK

Fur trade. In 1921 New York succeeded St Louis as the centre of the wholesale fur trade.

'As satin needlework'. George Shiras, third from the March, 1918, *Forest and Stream*, quoted by *The Literary Digest* of 30th March, 1918: 'Only once in the long period that I have hunted or photographed these animals (white-tailed deer) in this region have I seen an albino, and that one lingered for a year and a half about my camp, which is situated midway between Marquette and Grand Island. Signs were put up in the neighbourhood reading: "Do not shoot the white deer – it will bring you bad luck." But . . . it was killed by an unsuperstitious homesteader, and the heretofore unsuccessful efforts to photograph it naturally came to an end.

'Some eight years ago word came that a fine albino buck had been frequently seen on Grand Island and that it came to a little pond on the easterly part of the island. Taking a camping outfit, a canoe, and my guide, several days and nights were spent watching the pond; . . . the white buck did not appear.

'The next year the quest was no more successful, and when I heard that on the opening of the season the buck had been killed by a lumberjack, it was satisfactory to know that the body had been shipped to a taxidermist in Detroit, preparatory to being added to the little museum of the island hotel.

'About the middle of June, 1916, a white fawn only a few days old was discovered in a thicket and brought to the hotel. Here, in the company of another fawn, it grew rapidly. During the earlier months this fawn had the usual row of white spots on the back and sides, and although there was no difference between these and the body colour, they were conspicuous in the same way that satin needlework in a single colour may carry a varied pattern. . . . In June, 1917, one of these does bore an albino fawn, which lacked, however, the brocaded spots which characterized the previous one.

'It may be of interest to note that the original buck weighed 150 pounds and possessed a rather extraordinary set of antlers, spreading twenty-six inches, with terminal points much further apart than any I have ever seen. The velvet on the antlers . . . was snow-white, giving them a most statuesque appearance amid the green foliage of the forest. The eyes of the three native albinos are a very light gray-blue, while the doe has the usual red eyeballs.'

If the fur is not finer. Frank Alvah Parsons – *The Psychology of Dress* (Doubleday) – quotes Isabella, Duchess of Gonzaga: 'I wish black cloth even if it cost ten ducats a yard. If it is only as good as that which I see other people wear, I had rather be without it.'

'Accessibility to experience'. Henry James.

PEOPLE'S SURROUNDINGS

'Natural promptness'. Ward's *English Poets*. Webbe – 'a witty gentleman and the very chief of our late rhymers. Gifts of wit and natural promptness appear in him abundantly.'

'1420 pages'. Advertisement, *New York Times*, 13th June, 1921: 'Paper – As Long as a Man, As Thin as a Hair. One of the Lindenmeyr Lines was selected by Funk and Wagnalls Company, publishers of *The Literary Digest*, and *The Standard Dictionary*, for their twelve page pamphlet on India Paper. India Paper is so extremely thin that many grew fearful of the results when the unwieldly size, 45 × 65 inches, was mentioned. No mill ever made so large a sheet of India Paper; no printer ever attempted to handle it. But S. D. Warren Company produced the paper and Charles Francis Press printed it – printed it in two colours with perfect register. Warren's India is so thin that 1420 pages make only one inch.'

Persian velvet. Sixteen-century specimen in the exhibition of Persian objects, Bush Terminal Building, New York City, December, 1919, under the auspices of the Persian Throne: 'The design consists of single rose bushes in pearl white and pale black outline, posed on a field of light brown ivory so that the whole piece bears the likeness of the leopard's spots.'

Municipal bat-roost. Experiment in San Antonio, Texas, to combat mosquitoes.

Bluebeard's limestone tower at St Thomas, the Virgin Islands.

'Chessmen carved out of moonstones'. Anatole France.

'As an escalator cuts the nerve of progress'. The Reverend J. W. Darr.

'Captains of armies', etc. Raphael: *Horary Astrology*.

'The slight snake', etc. George Adam Smith: *The Expositor's Bible*.

MARRIAGE

'Of circular traditions'. Francis Bacon.

Write simultaneously. *Scientific American*, January, 1922, 'Multiple Consciousness or Reflex Action of Unaccustomed Range': 'Miss A—— will write simultaneously in three languages, English, German, and French, talking in the meantime. (She) takes advantage of her abilities in everyday life, writing her letters simultaneously with both hands; namely, the first, third, and fifth words with her left and the second, fourth, and sixth with her right hand. While generally writing outward, she is able as well to write inward with both hands.'

'See her, see her in this common world'. 'George Shock'.

'Unlike flesh, stones', etc. Richard Baxter: *The Saints' Everlasting Rest*.

'We were puzzled and we were fascinated, as if by something feline, by something colubrine.' Philip Littell, reviewing Santayana's Poems; *New Republic*, 21st March, 1923.

'Treading chasms'. Hazlitt: *Essay on Burke's style*.

'Past states'. Richard Baxter.

'He experiences a solemn joy'. 'A Travers Champs', by Anatole France in *Filles et Garçons* (Hachette): 'le petit Jean comprend qu'il est beau et cette idée le pénètre d'un respect profond de lui-même. . . . Il goûte une joie pieuse à se sentir devenu une idole.'

'It clothes me with a shirt of fire'. Hagop Boghossian in a poem, *The Nightingale*.

'He dares not clap his hands'. Edward Thomas: *Feminine Influence on the Poets* (Martin Secker).

'Illusion of a fire', 'as high as deep'. Richard Baxter.

'Marriage is a law, and the worst of all laws . . . a very trivial object indeed.' Godwin.

'For love that will gaze an eagle blind', etc. Anthony Trollope: *Barchester Towers*.

'No truth can be fully known until it has been tried by the tooth of disputation.' Robert of Sorbonne.

'Darkeneth her countenance as a bear doth'. Ecclesiasticus.

'Seldom and cold'. Richard Baxter.

'Married people often look that way.' C. Bertram Hartmann.

'Ahasuerus' *tête-à-tête* banquet'. G. Adam Smith: *Expositor's Bible*.

'Good monster, lead the way.' *The Tempest*.

'Four o'clock does not exist.' The Comtesse de Noailles: *Femina*, December, 1921. 'Le Thé': 'Dans leur imperieuse humilité elles jouent instinctivement leurs rôles sur le globe.'

'What monarch', etc. From *The Rape of the Lock*, a parody by Mary Frances Nearing, with suggestions by M. Moore.

'The sound of the flute'. A. Mitram Rhibany: *The Syrian Christ*. Silence of women – 'to an Oriental, this is as poetry set to music.'

'Men are monopolists.' Miss M. Carey Thomas, Founder's address, Mount Holyoke, 1921: 'Men practically reserve for themselves stately funerals, splendid monuments, memorial statues, membership in academies, medals, titles, honorary degrees, stars, garters, ribbons, buttons and other shining baubles, so valueless in themselves and yet so infinitely desirable because they are symbols of recognition by their fellow-craftsmen of difficult work well done.'

'The crumbs from a lion's meal'. Amos iii. 12. Translation by George Adam Smith, *Expositor's Bible*.

'A wife is a coffin.' Ezra Pound.

'Settle on my hand.' Charles Reade: *Christie Johnston*.

'Asiatics have rights; Europeans have obligations.' Edmund Burke.

'Leaves her peaceful husband.' Simone Puget: an advertisement entitled 'Change of Fashion', *English Review*, June, 1914. 'Thus proceed pretty dolls when they leave their old home to renovate their frame, and dear others who may abandon their peaceful husband only because they have seen enough of him.'

'Everything to do with love is mystery.' F. C. Tilney; *Fables of La Fontaine*, 'Love and Folly', Book XII, No. 14.

'Liberty and Union.' Daniel Webster (statue with inscription, Central Park, New York City).

NOVICES

'Is it the buyer or the seller who gives the money?' Anatole France: *Petit Pierre*.

'Dracontine cockatrices'. Southey: *The Young Dragon*.

'Lit by the half lights of more conscious art.' A. R. Gordon: *The Poets of the Old Testament* (Hodder and Stoughton).

'The smell of box, although not sweet, is more agreeable to me than many that are. . . . The cypress too seems to strengthen the nerves of the brain.' Landor: *Petrarca*, in the *Imaginary Conversations*.

'The Chinese objects of art and porcelain dispersed by Messrs. Puttick and Simpson on the 18th had that tinge of sadness which a reflective mind always feels; it is so little and so much.' Arthur Hadyn: *Illustrated London News*, 26th February, 1921.

'The authors are wonderful people.' Leigh Hunt.

'Much noble vagueness'. James Harvey Robinson: *The Mind in the Making*.

'Split like a glass against a wall'. *The Decameron*, 'Freaks of Fortune'.

'Precipitate of dazzling impressions'. A. R. Gordon.

'Fathomless suggestions of colour'. P. T. Forsyth: *Christ on Parnassus* (Hodder and Stoughton).

'Ocean of hurrying consonants', 'with foam on its barriers', 'crashing itself out'. George Adam Smith: *Expositor's Bible*.

'Flashing lances', 'molten fires'. *The Autobiography of Leigh Hunt*.

AN OCTOPUS

Glass that will bend. Sir William Bell, of the British Institute of Patentees, has made a list of inventions which he says the world needs: glass that will bend; a smooth road surface that will not be slippery in wet weather; a furnace that will conserve 95 per cent. of its heat; a process to make flannel unshrinkable; a noiseless airplane; a motor-engine of one pound weight per horse-power; methods to reduce friction; a process to extract phosphorus from vulcanized indiarubber, so that it can be boiled up and used again; practical ways of utilizing the tides.

'Picking periwinkles'. M. C. Carey: *London Graphic*, 25th August, 1923.

'Spider fashion'. W. P. Pycraft: *Illustrated London News*, 28th June, 1924.

'Ghostly pallor', 'creeping slowly'. Francis Ward: *Illustrated London News*, 11th August, 1923.

'Magnitude of their root systems'. John Muir.

'Creepy to behold'. W. P. Pycraft; *Illustrated London News*, 28th June, 1924.

'Each like the shadow of the one beside it'. Ruskin.

'Thoughtful beavers', 'blue stone forests', 'bristling, puny, swearing men', 'tear the snow', 'flat on the ground', 'bent in a half circle'. Clifton Johnson: *What to See in America* (Macmillan).

'Conformed to an edge', 'grottoes', 'two pairs of trousers' – 'My old packer, Bill Peyto . . . would give one or two nervous yanks at the fringe and tear off the longer pieces, so that his

outer trousers disappeared day by day from below up-
wards. . . . (He usually wears two pairs of trousers)' – 'glass
eyes', 'business men', 'with a sound like the crack of a rifle'.
W. D. Wilcox; *The Rockies of Canada* (Putnam).

'Menagerie of styles'. W. M. 'The Mystery of an Adjective
and of Evening Clothes'. *London Graphic*, 21st June, 1924.

'They make a nice appearance, don't they?' Overheard at
the circus.

'Greek, that pride-producing language'. Anthony Trollope's
Autobiography.

'Rashness is rendered innocuous', 'so noble and so fair'.
Cardinal Newman: *Historical Sketches*.

'Complexities . . . an accident'. Richard Baxter; *The Saints'
Everlasting Rest*.

'The Greeks were emotionally sensitive.' W. D. Hyde: *The
Five Great Philosophies* (Macmillan).

Quoted lines of which the source is not given, are from
Department of the Interior Rules and Regulations, The Na-
tional Parks Portfolio.

SEA UNICORNS AND LAND UNICORNS

'Mighty monoceroses', etc. Spenser.

'Disquiet shippers'. Violet A. Wilson, in *Queen Elizabeth's
Maids of Honour* (Lane), quotes Olaus Magnus: *History of the
Goths and Swedes*, with regard to the sea serpent; says of Caven-
dish as a voyager, 'He sailed up the Thames in splendour, the sails
of his ship being cloth of gold and his seamen clad in rich silks.
Many were the curiosities which the explorers brought home as
presents for the ladies. The Queen naturally had first choice and
to her fell the unicorn's horn valued at a hundred thousand
pounds, which became one of the treasures of Windsor.'

Sir John Hawkins 'affirmed the existence of land unicorns
in the forests of Florida, and from their presence deduced

abundance of lions because of the antipathy between the two animals, so that "where the one is the other cannot be missing".'

Apropos Queen Elizabeth's dresses, 'cobwebs, and knotts, and mulberries'. 'A petticoat embroidered all over slightly with snakes of Venice gold and silver and some O's, with a faire border embroidered like seas, cloudes, and rainbowes.'

'In politics, in trade'. Henry James: *English Hours*.

'Polished garlands', 'myrtle rods'. J. A. Symonds.

The long tailed bear. In *Adventures in Bolivia* (Lane), p. 193, C. H. Prodgers tells of a strange animal that he bought: 'It was stuffed with long grass and cost me ten shillings, turning out eventually to be a bear with a tail. In his book on wild life, Rowland Ward says, "Amongst the rarest animals is a bear with a tail; this animal is known to exist, is very rare, and only to be found in the forest of Ecuador," and this was where the man who sold it to me said he got it.'

'Agreeable terror'. Leigh Hunt. 'The lover of reading will derive agreeable terror from *Sir Bertram and The Haunted Chamber*.'

'Moonbeam throat', 'with pavon high', 'upon her lap'. *Mediaeval*: an anonymous poem in *Punch*, 25th April, 1923.

An unmatched device. Bulfinch's *Mythology*, under 'Unicorn'.

Herodotus says of the phoenix, 'I have not seen it myself except in a picture.'

'Impossible to take alive'. Pliny.

'As straight'. Charles Cotton – 'An Epitaph on M.H.

> As soft, and snowy, as that down
> Adorns the Blow-ball's frizzled crown;
> As straight and slender as the crest,
> Or antlet of the one-beam'd beast;'

The Chili pine (araucaria imbricata). Arauco, a part of southern Chili.

'A certain proportion in the skeleton'. Lafcadio Hearn: *Talks to Writers* (Dodd, Mead).

INJUDICIOUS GARDENING

Letters of Robert Browning and Elizabeth Barrett (Harper), Vol. I, p. 513: 'the yellow rose? "Infidelity", says the dictionary of flowers'. Vol. II, p. 38: 'I planted a full dozen more rose-trees, all white – to take away the yellow-rose reproach!'

TO A SNAIL

'Compression is the first grace of style.' The treatise on rhetoric by Demetrius Phalereus, or a later Alexandrian?

'NOTHING WILL CURE THE SICK LION'

Carlyle.

TO THE PEACOCK OF FRANCE

'Taking charge', 'anchorites'. *Molière*: A Biography, by H. C. Chatfield-Taylor (Chatto).

THE PAST IS THE PRESENT

'Hebrew poetry is prose with a sort of heightened consciousness.' The Reverend E. H. Kellogg.

'HE WROTE THE HISTORY BOOK'

At the age of five or six, John Andrews, son of Dr C. M. Andrews, said when asked his name, 'My name is John Andrews; my father wrote the history book.'

'Water in motion is far from level.' *Literary Digest.*

SILENCE

'My father used to say, "Superior people never make long visits. When I am visiting, I like to go about by myself. I never had to be shown Longfellow's grave or the glass flowers at Harvard."' Miss A. M. Homans.

Edmund Burke, in *Burke's Life*, by Prior. '"Throw yourself into a coach," said he. "Come down and make my house your inn."'

Index